UNIVERSAL MONSTERS:

Origins

Christopher Ripley

Editor: Jan Davies
Layout & Cover Design: Emily
Additional Research: Kate Morgan
Special thanks go to James-Michael Roddy and to
Universal Studios' Archives and Collections Dept.

ISBN 978-0995536210
Address any queries to hhnunofficial@gmail.com

The author's dedication goes to Universal Studios, home to horror for over a century; long may you reign supreme and continue to create our nightmares…

UNIVERSAL MONSTERS: Origins

CONTENTS

UNIVERSAL MONSTERS: Origins

ACKNOWLEDGMENTS

The Author would like to thank the Halloween Horror Nights fan community, without your friendship, comradeship and passion this book would not have been created.

I thank you all and happy Halloween!

UNIVERSAL MONSTERS: Origins

"Listen to them, children of the night. What music they make…"

Those immortal words were first spoken by Bela Lugosi in a role that would identify him for the rest of his career. Dracula. That film opened on an unsuspecting audience in February of 1931.

The Prince of Darkness was quickly followed the same year by Frankenstein. The Mummy followed in 1932, then The Bride of Frankenstein in 1935, The Wolfman in 1941 and much later – The Creature From The Black Lagoon in 1954. For more than 85 years these have been there, in the dark, waiting to send terror down our spine. But as much as we fear them, we also are drawn to them.

The power of the Monsters is undeniable. Ask a child to play Frankenstein, and even though he or she has never seen James Whale's classic, they instinctively know to stretch out the arms and lumber towards you with a dead stare and cadaverous heaviness of a reanimated corpse.

I would argue that there is more an awareness of these characters than the Greek Gods Zeus, Aphrodite, and Illiad. In some cases, more people can describe the proper way to dispose of a Vampire or Werewolf than can recite any constitutional amendment or tell you who held the office of the twenty-sixth President of the United States.

These creatures of the dark are timeless. They still permeate our culture, although some would argue that their fear factor had lessened to a great degree. When we were developing Halloween Horror Nights: Ripped From The Silver Screen, one of our goals was to make these properties terrifying for a new audience. Frankenstein's Monster had become the comedic Herman Munster, and the pinkish Frankenberry, Dracula's bite had become

3

more sensual than sinister, and the Wolf-man was in danger of being de-fanged. So, we looked to the original films and the myths and legends that inspired them. There was the stuff of nightmares. The little details that when combined with imagination became unimaginable. And that is what Christopher has done with this book.

The Classic Monsters truly are our modern mythology. They are the simple stories that are handed down by the firelight of television and movies.

Of course, they were much more prevalent in the late sixties and early seventies when television horror hosts would fill the programming slots of late Friday night and Saturday afternoon with creature features. In my documentary Monsterkids, I set out to examine the cultural impact of the Monsters and the eternal man-child appreciation/infatuation. What began in the sixties and seventies is still going strong today, although the cast of creepy characters has certainly grown to include Michael Myers, Jason Voorhees, Freddy Krueger and Leatherface.

What was that spark of electricity, that inspiration that brought those creatures to life? What was the collection of elements that created the perfect ghastly story that would live on and on?

Universal Monsters Origins is a perfect primer. Christopher has done his homework (hopefully by candlelight, with a raging lightning storm outside) and delved into the catacombs to reveal the components of mythology, and in some cases cryptozoology, that inspired the ghastly grouping known as the Universal Classic Monsters. What is contained within the pages of this book is a deeper look at where these stories came from, whether it was a well-crafted tale of horror from Bram Stoker or Mary Shelley, or a myth handed down from an unfortunate encounter with a supernatural beast, or a cruel madman who used blood and terror to frighten his enemies.

4

100 years from now through the beauty of high definition, we will still have these films, and now, you will have the stories behind those stories. So sit back, and enjoy. Light your lantern, grab your Garlic and Wolfsbane and hold close as we set out to explore the shocking stories behind the stories.

Oh, and if you want to know, my favorite Classic Monster is the Frankenstein Monster. The combination of a truly ghoulish story filled with corpses and graveyards, along with James Whale's direction and Frank Pierce's epic make-up will live on and terrorize for many years to come.

James-Michael Roddy

Director of upcoming documentary *Monster Kids,*

Producer of *The Shark Is Still Working* and

Former *Halloween Horror Nights* Show Director.

The Beginning

For centuries the draw of horror tales have been vastly popular. People love to be scared. When silent films began in the late 1800s to early 1900s, it didn't take long for horror to become a staple. Without sound, having intricate sets, expressive acting and experienced directors were the perfect tools to convey scary and otherworldly topics.

Universal Studios was a giant at the time in terms of films, but particularly those of the horror genre. One by one they introduced films that explored the eerily uncomfortable and visually horrifying. Great actors stood out, wanting to take on roles that allowed them to play with makeup and lighting, as well as allowing them to act in dastardly and scary productions.

The Birth of Horror

The term "horror" was first realized by Horace Walpole in 1764. He released The Castle of Otranto, a supernatural thriller. Though it was not considered to be a literary masterpiece by any means, it did open the door for other writers to start exploring horror as a genre. Gothic novels were released but it wasn't until 1818 when Mary Shelley's Frankenstein was released that the movement of horror was officially noted.

From there, Emily Bronte introduced Wuthering Heights and Charles Dickens created a collection of ghost stories. Herman Melville also incorporated some horror and the supernatural into his masterpiece Moby Dick. As entertainment moved into the world of films, studios looked to the classics for inspiration and soon were creating silent films based on novels and commissioning writers to come up with their own supernatural tales.

Perhaps one of the very first official horror movies to enter the film market was The House of the Devil, which was released in Britain as The Devil's Castle in 1897. It was directed by Parisian film maker George Méliès, who was also known as a premier illusionist in his day. Possibly the combination of being a director who loved illusion made him the perfect candidate to create the film.

The film itself was a short and silent one. It showcases the story of a meeting with the devil and other fantasy spirits. If Méliès was shooting for terror, he fell short of the mark. Initially the film was amusing to its audience, rather than terror-inducing. The plot opens with a bat making its way to a monastic castle of the medieval era. It flies around until suddenly it morphs into the devil, or Mephistopheles. He, along with his assistant, use dark magic to create a woman. Two wealthy gentlemen enter the room, upon which the assistant pokes them in the back and then disappears, only to appear on the other side of the room. They are terrified and one runs. The other stays and the assistant continues to play more tricks on him. He makes a skeleton appear and he moves furniture around the room.

Despite the efforts to terrify the visitor, he remains unfazed. Mephistopheles and his assistant continue to try to scare the man. He fights the skeleton, but it then morphs into a bat, then into Mephistopheles. Four ghosts appear and then Mephistopheles turns the woman into a withered old witch and then into four ghosts again. Finally the man runs off, fleeing off a balcony. Mephistopheles appears in front of the man who finally brandishes a crucifix that causes him to disappear.

The House of the Devil was meant to be horror, but entertained its audience as a comedy. Still, it is credited as the first official horror movie because of its themes and characters. What was also notable about the film was Méliès' use of cinematography to morph characters into other characters. Though technology did not exist to create such visuals, Méliès used limited tools and his imagination to create a relatively impressive production.

Méliès' property was the setting for the film and he released it via his own company, the Star Film Company. The film was considered to be lost, until in 1988 when a copy was located. It is one of the most important contributions to the history of film due to its then-innovative style and the first horror-centric theme.

Another historical film that centered on this genre of horror was The Golem, as released in the United States with the title The Monster of Fate in 1915. It was directed by Henrik Galeen and Paul Wegener, and inspired by ancient legends from Judaism. This was the first film trilogy to enter the film market, as it was followed up in 1917 with The Golem and the Dancing Girl and then in 1920 with The Golem: How He Came into the World.

A scene from The Devil's Castle in 1897.

German-born Paul Wegener was known as an expressionist with his film style, and catered to the genre of horror for many movies throughout his career. Australian Henrik Galeen was another influential artist of the time. He began a life-long involvement in film in 1913 by writing various screenplays. Together the two horror artists produced The Golem, a story revolving around a statue that is brought mysteriously to life by a rabbi. He is found by an antique dealer who takes him as a servant. The Golem meets the dealer's wife and falls in love with her. His love, however, is unrequited and a string of murders occur throughout the land.

What is interesting about this contribution to horror history is the tie to a mystical statue that is imbued with human characteristics and is capable of human functions, including love. The character, played by Paul Wegener on film, retains his clay-like look throughout the film. It also is the starting point of a storyline that extended for five years, to the final installment of the trilogy.

The 60-minute long film was another silent era picture that relied solely on visuals to convey the storyline. This was limiting with the first films produced, so directors and writers had to rely heavily on the writing and the actors to communicate the plotline. The intricate scenery and luxurious setting also work to keep the audience on track with the story. What is notable also with this film is that it deals with the most tragic issues that people go through: love, unrequited love, passion, death and mystery. As an entrant into the notable films in horror history, it makes its best play for the title with its anthropomorphism of an inanimate object that wreaks havoc on society due to passionate love that is not returned.

Carl Mayer and Hans Janowitz wrote the silent film The Cabinet of Dr. Caligari and it was directed by Robert Wiene in 1920. This film came to be known as one of the top works of German Expressionism. The story's main character is a hypnotist who is insane. He influences a sleepwalker to start committing murders throughout the town. What is most startling about the film is that it uses a very unique visual style to convey its horror theme. Francis is the main character in the picture. He is discussing his life with another older man when a woman named Jane passes them by. Francis tells his companion that she is his fiancée. Much of the film is told from Francis' point of view and a reliving of past experiences via flashbacks. It starts off with Francis talking of his childhood home in Holstenwall, a village known for its dark, twisted streets and confusing layout. Francis and a young friend Alan compete for the affections of Jane. A visitor to the town, Mr. Caligari, brings a sleepwalker named Cesare to the fair as a sideshow, but needs a permit. The clerk who he requests the permit from berates him and mocks him, but eventually gives him the needed document. That night, the clerk is found dead in his bed.

The following morning when Francis, along with Alan, visit the sideshow, Mr. Caligari opens a coffin to reveal Cesare sleeping. The doctor orders him awake and says that he will answer any question an audience member has. Alan asks the sleeper how long he has to live. Cesare tells him he has until dawn. Later that same night, Alan is stabbed to death while in his bed. Francis tries to investigate the murder by enlisting help from Jane and Dr. Olsen, her father. They narrow down their search to a criminal brandishing a knife as he attempts to murder an old woman. Though he is caught and admits to trying to murder the old woman, he denies having anything to do with the other previous murders.

Francis then spies on the mysterious Dr. Caligari and sees Cesare sleeping in his coffin-like box. At the same time the actual Cesare goes to Jane's home and abducts her. An angry mob catch wind of the attempted abduction and chase the two. Cesare eventually lets Jane go and he flees. During his fleeing however he collapses on the street and dies. The police, along with Francis, investigate to find that Cesare who is in the box is just a dummy. Dr. Caligari is chased by Francis, who is led to an insane asylum.

Francis learns that the doctor is the director of that asylum. He investigates and realizes the doctor is obsessed with the tale of an 18th century mystic who was named Caligari and used a sleepwalker named Cesare to murder townspeople. The doctor is apprehended by the police and ultimately ends up as an inmate within his own asylum. The storyline returns to present time where Francis reveals a twist-ending. Francis is actually an inmate of the asylum. Both Cesare and Jane are patients—Jane being delusional and Cesare being dangerous. Dr. Caligari is the asylum director but Francis attacks him. They eventually are placed in the same cell and the doctor announced that he can cure Francis.   What is interesting to note about this film is its unique-to-the-time flashback characteristics and its plot-twist ending. Both solidify its place in horror as a cutting edge and unique film that opened the door of possibilities for writers from that time on.

A still from the 1920 production of The Cabinet of Dr. Caligari

Germany, which had produced these new gothic pictures was in many ways the center of the world's movie making industry. It would be a combination of war upheaval in Europe during these early decades and Edison's loss of sore patents to the movie camera in America that gave birth to Hollywood. Many Germans escaping persecution in Europe and many American wanting to work in film all left for Los Angeles to create a new center of filmmaking for the world. It was this creation of Hollywood in the early twentieth century that would see the genre of horror (or thriller as it was known then) come to great fruition. It was one particular Jewish immigrant, Carl Laemmle, who founded his own studio, that of Universal Studios in 1912, who could go on to bring the horror genre to new *frightening* heights.

In 1923 The Hunchback of Notre Dame was released by director Wallace Worsley. It starred Lon Chaney, considered to be one of the era's more powerful actors. He was known for portraying characters who were tortured and for using makeup to portray their sufferings. The film was produced and distributed by Universal Studios and was the most successful silent film they had ever released, bringing in more than $3m at the box office; which for the time was a staggering amount of money.

The story is based on the novel of the same name by Victor Hugo from 1831. The year was 1482 when Quasimodo, the deaf and partially blind hunchback, is tasked with ringing the Cathedral of Notre Dame's bell in Paris. His master is named Jehan and tasks the hunchback with kidnapping Esmeralda, a dancing gypsy girl. Captain Phoebus rescues the girl from Quasimodo while Jehan runs off, leaving Quasimodo as the sole villain. Phoebus becomes enthralled with Esmeralda. The punishment for Quasimodo is public lashings in the square. During the punishment, he asks for water, which Esmeralda brings to him.

Phoebus' intention to marry Esmeralda is found out by Jehan, and his brother Clopin. Phoebus is already engaged, however, to Fleur de Lys. Phoebus brings the gypsy girl to a fine ball and presents

13

her with linens, and riches. He introduces her as the Princess of Egypt. Clopin and Jehan break into the party and demand that Esmeralda be let go. Esmeralda admits she is not royalty and sends a poet to tell Phoebus she is not in love with him. Phoebus arrives to meet her but is stabbed by Jehan while on the way. Esmeralda is falsely accused of the murder but Quasimodo rescues her from the gallows. The two go to the cathedral and is granted sanctuary. Later, Clopin goes to the castle to take Esmeralda. A fight ensues and Quasimodo ends up throwing Jehan off the roof of the tower. He is fatally shot, however, and rings the bell signifying his own death.

A scene from the 1923 version of The Hunchback of Notre Dame

As a horror film, The Hunchback of Notre Dame is a notable one due to its creation of a monster, the monster's humanity, and the tragic ending. It was in 1922 when Universal Studios announced the movie and the inclusion of Lon Chaney as its star. As Chaney was known already for playing tortured characters, this was the perfect vehicle for him at the time. Universal's publication, Universal Weekly, announced in September of 1922 that this appearance would be Mr. Chaney's "final" role of a tortured soul. Throughout the remainder of the year, Universal Studios would release more and more information on the film, signifying just how big they believed it would be. Laemmle's instincts paid off, more than any other genre the studio had worked on, the horror genre would be the one that would throughout the years would pay the biggest dividends. Laemmle, quick to act, announced that another such picture should be worked on by the studio with much of the same ingredients. This picture would be The Phantom of the Opera which was released in 1925. This also starred big-name actor Lon Chaney in the title role. This was during the time that the film studio was a standout in the genre of horror. This new movie was another important contribution that solidified Universal's reputation as not only the now leader of their industry but also the home of horror pictures.

The Phantom of the Opera opens at Paris Opera House where Christine is the featured player. Vicomte Raoul visits her and asks her to retire and become his bride. She refuses. Management of the opera house tell new workers that there is a mysterious opera ghost who requests opera box #5. New managers believe it is a ruse. After a performance, ballerinas see a mystery man who is believed to live in the cellar beneath the opera house. They aren't sure he is the phantom, so they ask a stagehand who has seen the ghost. He paints a picture of a ghastly figure with a skeleton-like stance to him. Carlotta, the prima donna of the opera, storms into the manager's office angered that the Phantom has delivered her a letter telling her that Christine will be playing the lead role the following night. The voice heard tells Carlotta that there will be dire consequences if she refuses.

Raoul meets with Christine again to ask her to reconsider his proposal. She admits that she has heard a divine voice called "The Spirit of Music" and it is impossible for her to stop her career.

Carlotta falls ill that night and Christine sings. The workers look to box #5 to see who is in it. They are frightened to see a shadowy figure in the box. They immediately run out, but soon return and find it empty. Raoul comes to Christine's dressing room and hears her talking with someone. The voice tells her that he wants her love. Raoul sees her leave and goes into the dressing room to investigate but finds no one there.

Lon Chaney in the full makeup he devised for the tortured Phantom

Carlotta receives another note via the Phantom telling her that she will allow Christine to have her part. This time, Carlotta refuses and appears on stage. A crystal chandelier falls into the audience. Christine rushes to her dressing room and hears the mysterious voice. In an almost trance-like state, she is taken down into the lower depths of the Opera House and recalls moving on a gondola over the lake with the Phantom. The Phantom states his name is Erik. Christine notes his mask and sneaks up behind him, rips it off and sees his deformed face. Erik is furious and tells her he is going to keep her prisoner. He changes his mind, but notes that she is never allowed to see Raoul again. She agrees and is released. Of course the film ends with tragedy, as was the style of horror at the time. The Phantom is killed and Christine and Raoul end up on their honeymoon.

Universal Studios was behind the project from the beginning in 1911. Carl Laemmle, who was the president of the studio, received a copy of the novel and realized quickly that it was the perfect tool to give to Lon Chaney. What made the film so unique and groundbreaking was its use of makeup. Chaney was able to create a truly horrifying look for his Phantom. It is rumored when the film debuted, audiences fainted and some screamed at the visual Chaney created (there was no makeup artists for Chaney; he did all his own makeup and costuming. Some say he was as gifted in that field of work as he was at playing the freaks he created). There were some production issues, these were overshadowed by the gross box office of more than $2m, which again was a huge sum for this time.

The Cat and the Canary was another silent era horror production distributed by Universal Studios. At the time Universal was developing itself as the biggest name in horror and this film was considered its "cornerstone" production of the time. This film opens in a decaying mansion owned by Cyrus West, a millionaire with a greedy family. His family soon pounces upon him much like the title suggests and it drives him to insanity. He writes his last will and testament but orders that it remains under lock and key until twenty years after his death. Twenty years later his lawyer realizes a second will has materialized. The second comes with orders that it can only be opened if the first one's terms are not met. Caretaker of the mansion, Mammy tells the lawyer that the second document was placed by the ghost of West.

As the clock ticks down to the appointed day when the will is read, West's relatives come to the mansion. That day they find out that he left his fortune to a distant relative, Annabelle, who, as a requirement to receive the funds, must be deemed sane by doctor Ira Lazar. If Annabelle is deemed insane, then the fortune is passed to the second in line. Annabelle realizes that since she is first in line for the riches, now the relatives are chasing her, again like the title of the movie.

Suddenly a guard announces that there is a lunatic loose on the property and his reputation holds that he is like a "cat" who is chasing people like "canaries." In fact, he is referred to as "The Cat." Mr. West's lawyer, Mr. Crosby tells Annabelle that there is someone in line after her and she should be careful because he believes the family may try to harm her. As he is informing her, a hand with long nails comes out of a secret passage way and drags him in. Annabelle tried to tell her family what happened to the lawyer, but they decide that she is indeed insane.

Annabelle later finds a note that tells her where the jewels are in the form of a dazzling necklace. She finds the secret hiding place; a removable panel by the fireplace. She returns to her room and sleeps in the necklace. The hand with long nails once again appears as she is sleeping and takes the necklace off of her. The following day Annabelle and one of West's nephews, Harry, search the room but all they find is the secret passage in the wall. Here they find Crosby's dead body.

Manny calls the police while Annabelle and Paul go to her room and discover that Crosby's body is now gone. Paul then vanishes into the secret passageway. He is attacked by "The Cat" but regains consciousness just as Annabelle is in danger. He rescues her. The police arrive and capture "The Cat." They find out that "The Cat" actually was West's other nephew who was hoping to prove Annabelle mad and gain the inheritance.

As hoped by Universal Studios, the film was a success. They handed directorial duties over to Paul Leni because they knew that likely he would turn it into a film suitable for an American audience, using expressionist techniques. At the time, American audiences loved horror films and the style played well to that. Expressionist films were known to have asymmetric sets, intricate designs and over-the-top stylization included in the background. Add to that a horror storyline and great actors and it was a recipe for success. As expected, when it was released in New York City, it was a box office smash yet again for the fledgling company.

Director Paul Leni took the reins again with The Man Who Laughs in 1928, another Universal Picture production. This time, it was based on the writings of Victor Hugo. Despite some issues with the storyline, the theme of a disfigured man stayed with the movie industry. It is said that the Joker, of the highly successful Batman series of comics and films, was inspired by the movie's main character (the similarities are astounding).

The film takes place in England in 1690. Main character Gwynplaine offended the ruler at the time, King James II. His father is sentenced to death and Gwynplaine is punished by having Dr. Hardquannone disfigure his face into a grin. Homeless, Gwynplaine discovers a baby girl named Dea who is abandoned. They are both taken in by Ursus. Eventually when they grow older, Gwynplaine falls in love with Dea but she tells him his face is disfigured and she can never marry him. They end up making money by performing plays that showcase Gwynplaine's disfigurement and the city's fascination with is deformity.   One day they perform for Queen Anne, who took the throne after King James' death. She realizes that Gwynplaine has an inheritance coming to him. The estate of his father was taken over by Duchess Josiana. Queen Anne decrees that the Duchess must marry Gwynplaine. Josiana meets him and is attracted to him, but is still put off by his disfigured face. Gwynplaine refuses to marry her and escapes, as guards chase him. He located Ursus and Dea and they all escape on a boat.

Conrad Veidt depicted above in The Man Who Laughs had also starred in The Cabinet of Dr. Caligari

At the time Universal Studios was dominant in the genre of horror, having produced many successful films. The Man Who Laughs was another victory at the box office. Tapping Leni to direct was also part of the reason for its performance. Leni was well versed in the genre and knew well how to captivate and scare an American audience. He knew what they wanted in terms of horror and had the resources and expertise to deliver. Universal made headlines at the time, however, because he ordered the budget for the film to be well over $1m, which was largely unheard of at the time.

What made this film different for Universal Studios however is that it was largely panned by critics upon its first run. They stated that it was not true to the time period of 1690 visually, and that it was too morbid. Despite its criticisms, the film still made the motion picture company a good deal of revenue and solidified its place in the annals of classic films of the expressionism era. The investment didn't pay off as much as Universal had wanted, though by this time it had shown the industry that Universal was definitely one of the main players. They would continue to produce movies from this genre to varying degrees of investment and success, though it would be the 1930s when the genre would finally come into its own and prove that Universal was most definitely the home of horror.

DRACULA

"But first, on earth as vampire sent,

Thy corpse shall from its tomb be rent:

Then ghostly haunt thy native place,

And suck the blood of all thy race;

There from thy daughter, sister, wife,

At midnight drain the stream of life;

Yet loathe the banquet which perforce

Must feed thy livid living corpse:

Thy victims ere they yet expire

Shall know thy demon for their sire,

As cursing thee, thou cursing them,

Thy flowers are withered on the stem."

"The Giaour" (1813), Lord Byron

Vampire lore

The story of the vampire has been around for thousands of years; passed down from generation to generation to inform and educate the youngsters of what might occur should they come face to face with a bloodsucking "vampir." The earliest known references to vampires come from the ancient worlds of Egypt and Greece where demons that had been summoned from other worlds had been brought into our own to do the bidding of devious sorcerers.

Other than these vague tales from the ancient world, the story and origin of the vampire appears to be unique to every place the tale is told, and unlike many other ghoulish incarnations, the story of the vampire appears to be told in every corner of the planet. The most well-known story of them all is by far that of Dracula, with this account supposedly inspired by that of Vlad the Impaler.

Vlad, who had ruled portions of modern day Romania, was a respected ruler of the district and was known for impaling the heads of his defeated foes, though the nickname of "Impaler" was only applied posthumously and much later. His official title was that of Vlad III Dracula of Wallachia and ruler of Transylvania, reigning in the late 1400s. Surviving accounts of the ruler are patchy and somewhat contradictory. Citizens of the time recount a generous leader who protected their boundaries from invaders and who was a pleasant ruler to his people.

Bran Castle in Romanina is colloquially known by the locals as Castle Dracula

Nearby recently-settled Saxons, however, paint a picture of a far more ruthless fiend who, they say, would not just defeat invaders but would punish them all by torture and death, cumulating in the impalements from whence his name derived. Some estimate that his victims numbered in the hundreds of thousands. Often these multiple impalements would be located at the boundaries of his territories to act as visual messages for would-be invaders. Some historians believe that Vlad actively drank and bathed in the blood of his enemies and would take great pleasure in doing so. Many of the tales surrounding Vlad are sketchy at best and completely fabricated at worst, but whatever the true nature of this man we can be certain that made a big impact on historians of the time (and recent historians too0 as a ruthless leader and a strong warrior.

Romanians had known of and lived with the tales of undead vampires for thousands of years. To this day, vampires are known as "the moroi," a wording that translates from Latin to "mort" or "undead" and from the Slavic to mean "a nightmare." Some regions also refer to the beasts as "strigoi," or "the living dead." Romanian folklore describes the creatures as witches with two hearts and two souls. They would seek to combine with other strigoi in the area to consume lonely people or farmers' livestock. They were often described as being corpses that had risen from the grave and needing the blood sucked from their victim in order to maintain their outer-worldly existence. A series of requirements surrounding the management of these deadly beasts were quickly set up. Often, birth defects of babies were a signal that when they passed away the child would often become a vampire. The same was believed to be true of the seventh child born within a family or a baby born to a pregnant mother who had seen a black cat walk across her path. The list was endless. The strongest of all superstitions surrounding the vampire was that of a person who had died an unnatural death (i.e. murder) or someone who had died before they could be baptized. It is likely that these two latter considerations were probably taken up more by the local churches, so were therefore given more credence. Folklore also dictates that vampires would attack victims from behind before aiming to bite the still-beating heart or face of their victims. Through the centuries, sudden deaths, mysterious deaths, murders, or the eradication of an entire herd of livestock would all be blamed on the vampire. This would eventually lead local communities to check frequently on their recently deceased to ensure they had not succumbed to vampirism. Graves would be repeatedly checked to ensure they had not been disturbed, with a number of suspected bodies being exhumed followed by being washed, blessed and reburied.

The vampire is true, global phenomenon and folklores from around the world have all had their own versions of the much-feared undead demon. Other parts of Eastern Europe and Russia would recount the tale of the bloodsucking Mora, a female vampire that would strike only at the men that had crossed her. Other local legends would say the vampire could morph into a variety of animals, from the conventional bat to the pretty butterfly. Other female forms of the legend include the "Dearg-due," which translate from Gaelic as "Red Blood Sucker." She was supposedly a young and beautiful woman who commits suicide when forced into marriage. She would then rise from the grave and exact revenge on her father and her would-be husband. A similar tale is also told in Portugal where the female vampire would also take the form of birds and inflict injury on passing travelers or anyone that had crossed the being. Revenge seems to be a strong theme for many of the fables. One such tale from 1672 focuses on an area of Europe that is now a part of modern-day Croatia. There was mass panic amongst the villagers of a small settlement near Tinjan when a deceased peasant reportedly returned from the grave after some twenty years to exact punishment on his widow. He supposedly drank her blood and sexually harassed her before residents banded together to drive a stake of wood through his heart. The mayor of the village, on witnessing the horror, ordered that he be beheaded instead as the stake would likely fail. It would be these and countless other ancient myths that would fascinate and inform people for years, though it would be around this period when the legend would soon spread.

The legend of vampires is alive throughout the entire world. Almost every country has their own theory and history about the undead. It all seems to have begun, though, with Lilith. From ancient Mesopotamia, she was the earliest of the blood-sucking creatures who live off of humans. Originally known as Lamatsu, a (male) serpent demon who grabbed innocent children from their homes and ate them, he also was blamed when infants were found unresponsive and dead in their cribs. The male Lamatsu eventually turned into the female Lilith.

Lilith was found in early Hebraic writings. She was initially described as a winged demon that appeared in the body of a woman, but had talons as feet. Legend has it she was Adam's original wife and pre-dated Eve. She was formed just as Adam was - from dirt - by God, and refused to submit because she believed she was equal to her male counterpart. Because of her refusal to submit, God banished her from the Garden of Eden and she was sent to the demon realm. There she became known as "Mother of Demons."

Once she took on her title, Lilith carried on with her mischief. Legend claims that she began stealing infants from their cribs and small children from their beds to destroy them. She also targeted men in the form of a "succubus." A succubus was a woman who seduced men, to steal their life essence. Of course, by doing this she also killed them. Later versions of the legend stated that she also drank their blood when she was done with them. This is how she also produced offspring.

Lilith is believed to be the earliest vampire that history has given the world. After she was banished, God destroyed all of her children. This caused her to vow to feed off of children for all of eternity, beginning with Adam's future offspring. Her title "Mother of Demons" evolved into "Mother of Vampires."

Lilith's legend was a mainstay in the world. Regardless of country, there was always some account of vampires and their terrible actions. Regardless of their incarnation, there were commonalities between them: the vampire drank blood, was able to change shape, could lure its prey, and killed the innocent. Here are some popular vampire legends from around the world:

Germany has quite a few vampire legends. There is a popular Germanic spirit who is equitable to the "boogeyman" or an impish ghost. They believe that he torments the dreams of women. It is thought that this spirit comes when a relative passes away. His or her spirit turns into the spirit and visits. Interestingly enough, this legend has evolved. In the Middle Ages, the spirit was said to be an animal taking spirit form. It was variously reported as a bird, pig or cat. Werewolves were closely associated with the spirit animal because of their canine qualities and sleek movement ability.

Scotland too has its own version of a vampire, but it's a far cry from Germany's. In Scotland it's a Bao Bahan-sith, a vampire able to disguise itself in the body of a lovely young woman. She tempts victims and eventually leads them to their untimely deaths. The commonality of all her murders is that she is always wearing green when she lures people to their end. As legend has it, victims are drained of their blood and their corpses usually disappear.

The Irish historians also claim a vampire legend. Here, the vampire is Lamia, a beautiful fairy princess. Like BaoBahan-sith, she used her beauty to tempt men and lure them under her own charming spell. With her, though, it was lovemaking that drained men's life away until they died. There also is another legend of vampire proportions. It's the Dearg-due. This ancient vampire has been feared since back in the Celtic era. The only way to "kill" him is to determine which dead soul is hosting the beast, find their grave and pile heavy stones on top of it. This was thought to be the only way to rid a person of the vampire, but it was a long shot to find out who exactly was hiding it in the first place.

In Poland they have the Upier. This is a vampire that gets up in the middle of the day and torments people until midnight, when he is called back to his grave. The legend has it that he sleeps in a pool of blood and uses his daylight hours to seek large amounts more. Polish vampires never had just one form, though. The legend made the creature able to take on a wide range of forms. This shape shifting is what gave it its power and made everyone a potential victim.

Grecian vampires are also rife throughout the world of legends. In this country the imp took the form of a red-eyed monster who had the body of a woman but the lower body of a winged snake. This legend quickly took hold not just in Greece, but throughout Hungary, Transylvania and the Mediterranean areas. It is thought that the legend spread from China, India and Tibet when they were importing their fine textiles. Though legends began in Asian countries, they quickly took hold in European countries. The change was their red-eyed look though; it gave them the ability to see into a victim's soul and see what their true desire was. Having this knowledge, they could then use this to lure them in.

In India, people created the legend of the Rakshasa. This is a cat-like creature that walks upright like humans and dresses in fine clothing. Though this is a common form, it can take on many other forms, too. It can be a beautiful woman, or a tiger or a half-and-half creature such as half tiger, half man. They are said to hide in trees to target their victims. According to legend, they have the ability to cause illness and other magical powers to make trespassers sorry they came. This magic ability gives them their power because they can fool just about anyone into falling into their hands.

In Japan, they have the Gaki. These are white-skinned and cold beings that are similar to the American vampire legend. They can also transform themselves into different shapes and lure people. The difference though is that beyond animals, they can also transform themselves into any person they want. Having the skill to impersonate someone lets them target whomever they want for their next meal. It is said that they also have the power to become invisible and stalk their prey that way. What makes this legend unique is their ability to be a doppelganger as it opens the door to even more victims. It allows them to take on a specific notable shape and lure just about anyone to their demise.

In the Philippines, the vampire is the Aswang. It is a creature that appears at first as a beautiful woman. She has the ability to sound like a song bird at night. With a long tongue, she manages to drink the blood of her victims. Part of the legend is that she feeds on the blood of children only. It is her songlike call though that sets her apart from other legends. At night, the beauty of her call is often a welcome sound to wanderers who are lost in the woods. They move towards the beautiful sound until they find what they think is help.

Vlad the Impaler or Vlad Dracula, the inspiration for the world's most famous vampire.

In the western world, vampires are more sensationalized. They are akin to the Interview with a Vampire characters that Tom Cruise and Brad Pitt brought to life on the screen. They are to be feared, but they also are fine looking noblemen who rub shoulders with those of high society and noble upbringing. The dark side however is that they lure innocent people in order to drink their blood.

It would seem that by the eighteenth century that the epicenter for vampiric monsters would be Eastern Europe, as the lands of this area appeared to have the widest variety and quantity of different vampire tales. By this time the reports and legends would soon filter into western Europe, particularly Britain and Germany, where the tales were quickly popularized and overstated. This in return would see the vampire sightings and incidents of Eastern Europe significantly increase to epidemic proportions, and soon led to pockets of hysteria right across the continent. One of the first publicized panics came from Eastern Prussia (modern day Germany) where in 1721 an alleged spate of vampire attacks occurred from recently deceased persons apparently rising from the grave to drink the blood of the people they once knew.

These collective events would be known as "the eighteenth century vampire controversy," where a series of well-documented governing officials would write about the events and report on their findings at a state level. The news that drove the hysteria would last for nearly all of that century and would be exacerbated by a number of small outbreaks of various diseases and by a number of mostly rural superstitions. This would lead the church to become more involved with the study of vampirism, which seemed to quell the fears of the continent but would ultimately prolong belief in the legends. It would be these tales that would filter into the next century, that of the Romantic Period when the first tales of the vampire would be formally composed for the mass market; these books would certainly fuel the then vampire craze of the day. By the late nineteenth century, the stories and sightings of such mythological fiends had seriously cooled down, though it would be in 1897 when the legend would come back with a serious bite!

"From my grave to wander I am forced

Still to seek the God's long sever'd link,

Still to love the bridegroom I have lost,

And the lifeblood of his heart to drink."

"The Bride of Corinth" (1797) by Johann Wolfgang von Goethe.

There are some famous historical people who were thought to be vampires too. Elizabeth Bathory was one. She was born in 1560 in Transylvania. It was a desire to remain young that pushed her into trying a number of unconventional beauty remedies, one being drinking blood. Convinced that it was working, she became obsessed with blood and was thought to have murdered more than 600 young girls throughout her lifetime.

Another legendary vampire with a real background was Arnold Paole. He was born near Belgrade in the early 1700s. He was worried about dying at a young age; obsessively worried. A tragic farming accident left him bedridden and he died a few weeks later. During the time he was at home, townspeople reported seeing him in their homes. Soon after, a spate of deaths began in the town. They decided to exhume Arnold's body. When they did, the body was not decomposing at all - in fact, it looked like a human body. The wounds he suffered from his fall when he was alive had healed up. There was fresh blood on his lips. The townspeople put a stake through his heart and Arnold sat up and screamed.

Regardless of the legend, there is also a way to find a vampire's grave. It is done by having a seven-year-old boy ride a horse through the graveyard. When the horse stops, that's the grave of the vampire. The legend varies slightly throughout region though. In the northern part of Europe it has to be a naked virgin on the horse.

Whether or not vampires really exist, they are definitely a mainstay in history. From Lilith to Vlad to the popular Lestat, they make for fantastically scary stories to share. Their longstanding history has to beg the question though: if they aren't real, why has the legend managed to last for centuries?

The Novel

Bram Stoker had been building a well-established managerial career in the theatre. His business acumen combined with his love of drama and art to form a pleasant income for him and his family. Being born in Ireland and then subsequently moving to London, he would work with some of the great and good of Victorian society before accepting an appointment as business manager at the Lyceum Theatre located in the City of Westminster, a role in which he would work for nearly twenty years. The pay was humble and afforded him a suitably middle-class existence, but Stoker was not satisfied. Having formerly been appointed as personal assistant to Henry Irving (the theatre's then owner) and socializing with the likes of Oscar Wilde, Sir Arthur Conan Doyle (to whom he was distantly related), Rudyard Kipling, Robert Louis Stevenson, and the famed beauty Florence Balcombe, whom he later married, he felt he needed to do more with his life, and it was this inclination that spurred Stoker to begin writing. It was with Irving in 1890 that he visited the pleasant seaside town of Whitby, and it was here that the first inspirations for his coming works begin to churn within his being. It would be the journey home when he started to put pen to paper and form plot ideas and characterizations. Previously he had only written the odd chapter or short story for various periodicals, whereas now he had found his voice and drafted his first novel, that of The Snake's Pass. It was a suitably gothic affair that centered on St Patrick's battle to rid Ireland from snakes. The novel was mildly received, but it did what he wanted, which was to supplement his income and make a name for him in the creative realm. Spurred on by this reasonable success he started work on his next novel.

The real-life harbor of Whitby and the medieval ruins above are featured within the classic gothic horror novel

It was a chance meeting with Ármin Vámbéry during this time that gave Stoker the inspiration he required. Ironically, Stoker who had travelled the world with Irving had never been to any of the states and territories of Eastern Europe, so on meeting Vámbéry, Stoker became enchanted with the tales of European folklore, the tales of the Carpathian Mountains but most interestingly, the myth of the creeping vampire. Inspired by Vámbéry's tales and his former trip to Whitby he began researching and combining earlier plot ideas. This would lead him to visit the pleasant seaside town nearly every

summer during these years. At the time, the British Empire was at
its peak and it became fashionable to publish novels on topics that
could unseat the status quo. Many of Stoker's contemporaries were
writing about fantastical adventures set around the world and
romantic hero novels, and others were drafting speculative works
on the rise and fall of new technologies. Stoker would
intentionally pick ideas from every popular source material to aid
in his formation of his new book. There would be a hero, a
villain, and romantic notions but in a gothic setting. Stoker lined
up the ingredients as clinically as Conan Doyle had done in any of
his Sherlock Holmes stories. Though his book would not receive
legendary status initially it would over time grow to become one
of the most inspirational and genre-defining works of a lifetime.

During this time, he heavily researched Eastern Europe folklore
and from the chance meeting with Vámbéry he quickly became
obsessed with any and all vampire myths that he could find. He
even would have nightmares about vampires, and wrote positively
about one such experience from this time where he had eaten
seafood that was past its best. This supposedly caused him to fall
into a deep sleep where he dreamt of a "vampire king" that had
risen from the grave to do battle with the mortal. All of these
dreams formed ideas for the plot. He also took inspiration from
his boss Irving, carefully crafting the central character of his story,
the malevolent Count Dracula, after him. He did this intentionally,
in the hope that his boss might one day play such an easy part in
any future stage productions and therefore aid in the promotion of
his work; Stoker was after all a business manager at heart first. It
would be these gentlemanly mannerisms and an air of defined
class that would give such likeability to the enduring Count
Dracula.

Initially Stoker had set upon the name of The Dead Un-Dead,
which was later changed to The Un-Dead, and originally the name
of the Count was Count Wampyr. It fact the book name remained
this way during the years he worked on the novel, right up until a

few weeks before publication. Stoker had been researching Eastern European nobility when he stumbled upon a book called An Account of the Principalities of Wallachia and Moldavia with Political Observations Relative to Them by William Wilkinson, which he found in a library in Whitby. He became fascinated by the story of Drăculea, descendant of Vlad II of Wallachia, the name literally translating from Romanian as "the dragon" or "the devil." He took inspiration from his most famous descendant Vlad the Impaler where he anglicized their family name to the more familiar "Dracula," then changed a number of sections of the book, and finally revised the novel's name.

The book would become an epistolary novel, whereby it is an amalgamation of realistic diary entries, logs, letters, telegrams, newspaper clippings and the such that would all be presented in chronological order. Stoker, who by this time had become a part-time writer for the Daily Telegraph, seemed to enjoy this manner of writing. In total the original manuscript ran to 541 pages. At one point the original had been lost but was subsequently found in Pennsylvania in 1980s. It was seen that the handwritten title page was headed The Un-Dead in capital letters, but was subsequently crossed out (presumably by Stoker) with the inked Dracula written above. The manuscript was later sold to Microsoft co-founder Paul Allen.

The novel was not initially successful though it did provide Stoker with a reasonable income and a great deal of kudos. Published in 1897, it received largely positive praise with the then literary reviewer of the Daily Mail calling Stoker's work that of a genius that was far better than contemporary writers such as Shelley, Poe and Bronte; a bold statement indeed. It finally made its way across the ocean and was released in the US around 1899, being copyrighted that year in New York. Right before the release, Stoker created a play version of his book, which was still entitled The Un-Dead, but his former boss still refused to play the part that had been specifically inspired by Irving. Perhaps he thought the character was too familiar! Owing to little demand, the play was only performed once at his Lyceum Theatre.

The Lycheum Theatre in London's West End now home to Disney's Lion King was once the first theater to offer the play version of Dracula.

After Stoker's death in 1912 the popularity of the book picked up once more and began to become somewhat of a bestseller in pockets of the world. Stoker, who had died a relatively poor man, had not lived to see the success that would eventually be credited to his work. The success of the book combined with the new cinematic genre, where directors across the world were starting to take inspiration from the gothic noir book, particularly in Germany. The first movie to made on the story of Dracula was Dracula's Death, a 1921 Hungarian silent horror film that was written and directed by Károly Lajthay. The film was subsequently lost to time but did feature the very first adaptation of the novel. The film was not distributed widely and made little impact; it would be the next incarnation of the ruthless vampire that would make larger waves.

Germany by this time was the center of the world's movie-making industry. Many great luminaries would study here before going on to have long and successful careers, including the likes of Sir Alfred Hitchcock. It was local director F.W. Murnau who first approached Stoker's widow to obtain the film rights to her late husband's most famous work. The height of Dracula-mania was just commencing and Murnau knew he wanted to make this picture. Screenwriter Henrik Galeen was appointed to the picture and approached the Stoker estate. A flat "no" was received. Various further attempts were made until the production office decided to act without permission, suitably changing names and plot devices to ensure the work was "reminiscent" of the original. This included making the setting the 1830s rather than the 1890s and changing the location from England to Germany. In addition, character names were changed, new characters were introduced and the name of the main character of Dracula was altered to Count Orlok. This would create one of the first vampire movies ever, entitled Nosferatu. Despite various assurances, the film failed to avoid legal action. Florence, Stoker's widow, successfully sued the company and it was ruled that all copies of the movie be destroyed promptly (though some did survive). This garnered a lot of press attention and in return increased book sales tenfold across the world.

The public craved all things Dracula and vampiric by the mid-1920s. This led Florence to license the novel to playwright Hamilton Deane to create technically the second-ever version of the novel in play form. The Stoker family had known Deane for decades, so Florence was comfortable that he would do justice to her late husband's work. In 1924 the stage version was finally released. Initially touring before settling in London, Deane had originally intended himself to play the title role before opting to play the dogmatic Van Helsing. The original Dracula was played by famed English actor Raymond Huntley who stayed with the production on its relocation to London. The play played to packed-out audiences, the success was announced around the world and was soon noticed by Broadway producers. Horace Liveright brought the play to the US with sections of the script lightly revised to make it more appropriate for American audiences, and the title role this time was offered to a little known actor, Bela Lugosi.

The mysterious Count Orlok was played by Max Schrek in Nosferatu

Bela Lugosi was a young Hungarian-born actor who had been in Germany and witnessed the whole Nosferatu debacle (though he had nothing to do with this production) and had starred in a number of silent movies in Germany. He made a reasonable living here before leaving to start a new life in America. He arrived in the US in late 1920 via New Orleans before making his way to New York in early 1921. It was there in late March of 1921 that he was legally inspected for immigration at Ellis Island. He would later declare his intention to stay in the US in 1928, followed by becoming a citizen in 1931. The 6ft,1" tall actor initially made a living however he could, though laboring and manual jobs were all he could find. Entering into the Hungarian-settled communities of New York he soon banded together with other immigrant actors and formed a small company. This company would tour the Eastern seaboard playing to similar Hungarian community audiences, performing in their mother language.

 His first English speaking play was Red Poppy in 1921, which was presented on Broadway. More work soon came for the struggling actor, enough at least to drop his manual-labor jobs. Lugosi was working hard during this time to make enough money via his acting while trying to establish a name for himself in this English speaking dominated industry. In 1925 he played the part of an Arab sheik in Arabesque, a play which began in Buffalo, New York before moving to Broadway. This opened up a number of opportunities for the actor, affording him the chance to act in his first US silent picture, that of the 1923 melodrama The Silent Command. This would lead onto other similar roles, where the actor was starting to carve a reliable niche for himself as playing the foreign-sounding villains or untrustworthy continental Europeans. From this time onwards he was hardly out of work, managing to keep employed in various plays and films all shot in and around New York City. Then a telegram sent in the summer of 1927 changed Legosi's career forever.

Lugosi was their first choice to play the titular role of the new US-bound play of Dracula. On receiving an offer via telegram, he immediately accepted this once-in-a-lifetime offer and threw himself into his work. He read the original book and subsequent writings of the novel - literally everything he could source from the US to prepare for the role. The play would run to packed audiences and in total 261 performances were made on Broadway before the production toured across the US. The play generated both local and national headlines with a mild spatting of hysteria after a number of patrons fainted during the early performances, and as a result the production staff employed a doctor and nurses to attend all performances.

After a year of successful performances from East to West the production finished up in California, where the now burgeoning film industry of Hollywood was beginning to grow. Quick to see the opportunity in basing himself there, Lugosi relocated to Los Angeles where he was offered a role by Fox Studios to star in their next silent movie The Veiled Woman. Other film roles with the studios were forthcoming for the first few years, but then Hollywood's interest in Lugosi diminished. In 1929 he was let go by Fox and was offered the chance to reprise his most iconic role as the vampire count on a short tour of the play up and down the West coast. When the play ended Fox rehired the actor for the invention of new "talkies" that they had recently started to produce, again playing the quirky foreigner or just the exotic sounding villain. And although these roles paid the bills, his love affair with the Count was never far away. Lugosi was supposedly known to petition the Fox Studios to make his most iconic role into a movie, which Fox declined to do. Playing the Count on Broadway had been his most successful and critically acclaimed role ever and he largely grimaced at the chance to play Fox's villain of the week, though he would not need to wait too long for the chance.

In early 1930 the nearby Universal Studios began production of the successful play and initially wanted their horror leading man Lon Chaney to take the title role. Unfortunately for the production, Chaney suffered a hemorrhage and died shortly after the decision to bring the vampire story to the big screen.   Chaney, who was known for doing his own makeup and going back to the original source material to create his fantastical and grotesque characters, would surely have brought a different feel to the collective and sleek portrayal that Legosi would subsequently perform.

"The strength of the vampire is that people will not believe in him."

Van Helsing from Dracula (1931)

The Movie

Carl Laemmle Jnr immediately saw the potential for his studio to bring the Machiavellian count to the silver screen. Following careful research into how the Broadway contract had been agreed, he cautiously set about obtaining the full rights make a motion picture from both the novel and the play. He knew good business could be made from the horror genre as the box-office returns to the preceding pictures had been very lucrative for the studio. As the Broadway version had been a massive hit, they looked first at how the play had been constructed and used this as the basis for the movie. They also studied the silent and unofficial Nosferatu just for inspiration, along with comprehensive re-reading of the original source material. The movie would be an amalgamation of all the best elements, paying particular attention to the moments from the play that made the audience most react. One particular scene of note was the scene where Reinfield pricks his finger and the daring Count recoils in glee. This was a scene that proved very popular with audiences.

Lugosi was in the right place at the right time and one would assume that the actor who had made the Broadway play such a hit would be the front runner for the part, but he was not even considered in the top ten after Chaney's passing. Lugosi who had also taken up the role again on another touring version of the play lobbied the studio hard for the part, but was dismissed again ahead of other "bankable" stars. Other actors were approached with all of them passing on the part, with one actor supposedly telling Laemmle that the part should be Legosi's as no man on earth had put so much effort in researching the role than he. At the same time, Legosi's play was playing to great reviews and he used these to lobby the studio once again. Eventually the formidable Laemmle changed his mind and cast the actor in the main role, despite advice from his production staff. In return for winning the role Legosi was paid a meager salary compared to his contemporaries. Legosi would quip in later life that Laemmle only hired him after "everyone else in the phonebook turned the part down!" Along with Legosi, Edward Van Sloan starred as Van Helsing and Herbert Bunston as Doctor Seward, both of whom had reprised their roles from the famous Broadway version of the play.

Filming took place on the infamous backlot at Universal Studios in LA with a shoot that lasted just seven weeks. A number of accounts report that the production was a disorganized shoot, with the director Tod Browning, growing tired of a number of operational issues, leaving his cinematographer Karl Freund to direct the last couple of weeks (though Freund was never credited for this). Others have suggested that Browning may have been suffering from delayed mourning from the passing of his long friend Chaney. A scene where the ship is at sea was entirely scrapped after it proved too difficult to film, and instead stock footage from a silent movie shot on the backlot in 1925 was used with new sound effects. The footage had to be sped up to meet the pacing of the new talkie pictures and then edited effectively. All of these issues caused budgetary overruns.

The movie is not as lavish as past Universal horror productions, and in fact it reused sets that had already been built for other, recent productions. Rather than creating scores of new sets on parallel with the earlier productions, the production team decided to using the budget to recreate some of the special effects that had been successfully used in the play version. The smoke machines, special lighting and prop bats were a cheaper option than new sets, and even the costume that Lugosi wears on screen was his own costume.

A production still from the 1931 version of Dracula

These were also tight budgetary reasons for the production to keep it under a figure that was a lot less than the preceding Universal horror pictures. Some argue today that the earlier Depression had hit Universal Studio's coffers whereas other argue it was down to how Stoker had originally copyrighted the novel in 1899 in New

York City. It would transpire that Stoker had not fully complied with US copyright laws, which meant that portions of it would be classed as public domain. In the US and UK they follow the Berne Convention whereby an artist's work is theirs until fifty years after their death. This may have all led to Universal having to come up with addition funds to secure the project from the very beginning. Keen to see his most famous part reach the silver screen, Lugosi allegedly spoke to the widow of Stoker to aid in the negotiations, with some news outlets reporting that it was he that got the asking price down from $200,000 to $60,000 for Universal.

Commentators of the day also argued that Universal was taking a big gamble on releasing such a picture. Despite the literary and Broadway roots of the movie they argued that a full-length true horror picture with no comedic relief or trick ending would surely be too much for a then-prudish American audience. Whatever the reason, it was not known for sure why the movie's budget was so strict, though they need not have worried as the movie was about to become a global box-office smash hit. To date, adjusting for inflation, the 1931 movie has been one of the most successful versions of the novel ever made.

The movie premiered at the Roxy Theater in New York on February 12th 1931, and two days later it was released across the US. It caused a media frenzy when again audience members were reported to have fainted during the showing. This publicity drew attention yet again for these sensational reasons, all of which were stoked and then inflamed by the studio to ensure the film got as many column inches as possible. The earlier concerns of the movie proving too much handle were quickly wiped away when the box-office receipts appeared to be out-grossing every movie that Universal had ever made. A collective sigh of relief was heralded when 48 hours after opening the picture sold over 50,000 tickets at the theater where it premiered. The momentum continued to gather, with patrons just curious to see what all the fuss was about. This led the studio to reap a huge $700,000 profit, making it their most successful picture ever.

In 1931 censors were given little attention, but in 1936 when the film was re-released for a theatrical run the movie had two pieces of the original removed. Some of today's copies are from this 1936 revised version so it's worth pointing out what these two changes were. The first were the sound effects used when characters were killed. The groans were reduced and redubbed to make them less bloodthirsty. The other change was the removal of the original ending placement card, which read:

> *"Just a moment, ladies and gentlemen! A word before you go. We hope the memories of Dracula and Renfield won't give you bad dreams, so just a word of reassurance. When you get home tonight and the lights have been turned out and you are afraid to look behind the curtains — and you dread to see a face appear at the window — why, just pull yourself together and remember that after all, there are such things as vampires!"*

It was feared that religious groups might take exception to the notion that the studio was informing the public that such pagan demons actually existed. Unfortunately, it is said that the original end shot where this section is read is now lost forever.

> *"Dracula: You are too late. My blood now flows through her veins. She will live through the centuries to come...as I have lived."*

Dracula (1931)

The Spanish version

In the early days of cinema, it was entirely common for Hollywood studios to produce foreign language versions of movies they felt would sell well in specific territories. This was due to the fact that the technology to performing post-production dubbing had yet to be realized, and it was decided shortly before filming that a Spanish version should be undertaken. The film would be shot using the same equipment, props and sets as the English language version but all undertaken in the evenings and at night so as to not to disrupt the main production. This common practice would also see productions shot after hours in French, Italian or German for the European markets. This production would be directed by George Melford and would be entitled Drácula. As this version was done on a shoestring it was given little support to produce the movie, and in fact the actor picked to play the Count, Carlos Villarías, was the only member of the cast allowed on the set during the day. Melford wanted Villarías to try and imitate Legosi's performance so rather than set his own standard he was instructed to strictly portray the quirks and mannerisms of Legosi only. In order to save money some long shots of Legosi were used along with any sequences that had been made especially in post-production.

In more recent times the version has been bestowed with a fair amount of praise when it is compared to similar twilight productions made during this time. Unlike many other productions the Spanish crew had the luxury of being able to view the rushes from the following day; this enabled them to set up better camera angles or make more effective use of the special effects. Others point to the use of longer, suspenseful sections and a better attempt to edit a less well-paced version of the movie. In the end, the Spanish version would actually run to almost thirty minutes longer than the main version. These efforts for some sections of the movie prove to be better than the English version, an accolade that fairly was recognized in the foreign language versions. Some critics of more recent times have been bold enough to say that it is the superior of the two versions.

Carlos Villarías as Dracula in the Spanish Version of Dracula

The Spanish version was originally thought to be lost when the original production film was not located within Universal's vast archives. However, a print copy was discovered in the 1970s, which was later restored. In 2015 the Library of Congress selected this movie for preservation in the National Film Registry, citing that its contents were now artistically of merit enough for it to be saved for the nation.

The movie version of the famous vampire novel would effectively put Universal on the map and rise to parallel the book in importance. This, the first proper horror talkie, would tackle the supernatural in a way that had never been witnessed before. It established Universal as 'the home of horror' and would add great and permanent standing to the struggling movie studio. For its star, it would set the standard from which all portrayals of the famous Count have originated. Lugosi's iconic performance would inform the cultural zeitgeist for decades. Children to this day that have never seen this movie, when asked to describe what Count Dracula looks like, will always describe this iteration, proving that this movie is not just one of the most important movies from this genre but of all time too.

> *"What manner of man is this, or what manner of creature is it in the semblance of man? I feel the dread of this horrible place overpowering me; I am in fear — in awful fear— and there is no escape for me; 1 am encompassed about with terrors that I dare, not think of..."*

Jonathan Harker's Journal from Stoker's original Dracula.

The sequel

There was somewhat of a sequel to both the Dracula novel and the movie. His widow, Florence, released the book's sequel two years after Stoker's death in 1914. Both historians and academics have argued as to whether the book's sequel, entitled Dracula's Guest, was in fact a sequel to the original or, as many suspect, the "lost" first chapter. The short story is that of an unnamed Englishman who leaves Munich for an appointment with the bloodthirsty Count in Transylvania, where along the way he is attacked by a pack of wolves. Historians believe that the story is likely the first chapter that was allegedly scrapped by Stoker's publishers owing to the fact they felt it was superfluous to the overall narrative. Florence then set everyone straight by confirming:

"To his original list of stories in this book, I have added an hitherto unpublished episode from Dracula. It was originally excised owing to the length of the book, and may prove of interest to the many readers of what is considered my husband's most remarkable work."

Subsequent academics who have had access to the supposed original manuscript of Dracula have confirmed that evidence proves that the short story was the original lost chapter. There are also sentences later on in the book that are crossed-out as they refer to the attack from the wolves, such as Harker (the lead character) referencing the soreness from his neck following the attack.

Universal were a little late to the table when they decided to produce a sequel to what at this point had been their most profitable movie in the studio's fledgling history. The studio was still struggling financially and the requirement for a hit was no longer a nicety but a necessity. Initially, however, Universal thought they had been beaten to the punch, when news broke that rival Hollywood producer David O. Selznick had actually signed the rights to the book's sequel not long after their original movie had become the massive global hit that it became. Rumor had it that he was already working on a script that would see Harker travelling on the road to see the Count but is attacked by wolves which turn out to be the daughter of Dracula, a sort of prequel to the original movie. This enflamed Laemmle further as they had just had another hit with the sequel to Frankenstein, with The Bride of Frankenstein, whereby the feminized leading monster was popular with audiences, so for the shrewd Selznick to try and steal both concepts from under Universal's feet was incredibly audacious.

Selznick had one problem: he didn't own the rights to Dracula, so regardless of what he had purchased he would find it hard to proceed with his production without legal intervention from Universal, but the ever-astute Selznick knew this. He quickly hired John Balderston (who had a written a play version of the original book and had worked on a number of Universal pictures) to work on the new film. The secret term for the project was Tarantula, in order to keep Universal from knowing too much about what was unfolding. Balderston worked on the treatment and got the script to a filmic standard where the action focuses on the daughter of Dracula, with the actual title eventually becoming Dracula's Daughter. By this time Universal was threatening all kinds of action, when Selznick calmly called Laemmle and a deal was brokered. Nobody knows for how much but reports suggest that Selznick got far more for the deal than if he had simply sold the rights at the very beginning of the debacle. What Universal did not realize was that Selznick might not have been serious about making this picture. It was later found that Selznick had paid a mere $500 to Florence for the rights, so would Selznick have actually risked taking MGM into a lengthily and publicly damaging legal war over what was some say was really just a B-picture? The truth will surely never be known but the idea that Selznick was taking a "punt" is very likely.

The trouble though was not over for Universal, when in 1934 Universal, like all the other major studios, had to bow to pressure from the government, press and pressure groups over the control of censorship in their movies. This would herald the beginning of better regulation and control over what studios could and could not show in the cinemas, which would start from even before a script was finished. This would have a great impact on all future productions but would start with this movie.

Initially Laemmle hired James Whale, the successful director of the first two Frankenstein pictures, to work on the revised treatment that had been received from MGM. Whale's initial thoughts for the film were to take what MGM had presented but work more of their own Universal magic into the picture by bringing original cast members back in some form.

Presumably Whale was thinking of elaborating on the fact that Dracula was the undead after all, and there was uncertainty about whether Dracula actually got killed at the end of the film. Legosi was quickly approached and, as enthusiastic as ever, he agreed to star. Legosi, who had been paid a pittance for a movie that had become one of their largest ever grossing movies, was quick to point out that he would return but for a price; sentiments that the other cast members all shared. Whale presented his ambitions for the picture to Universal's board and was quickly slapped down for recklessly going around making promises for ideas for which he had no approval. They reminded the director that the Great Depression was still raging and Universal's expectations for this movie were along the lines of the original, that of a shoestring budget with the ambition of achieving maximum profits. Soon after Whale's dressing-down he quickly left the project, then word got around and none of the original cast and crew were interested either.

One actor was tempted back, that of Edward Van Sloan who had played the original Van Helsing. Universal's scriptwriters worked on the script and found that the most sensible place to pick the action up for the audiences would be to start the picture seconds after the ending of the original. The original's ending was a little abrupt and offered little resolution, so to start the feature here would make sense. In order to achieve this, they would need to bring back Van Sloan but could easily offer up Harker's leaving and just put carefully crafted dummies in the coffin to represent the dead vampires, including Legosi's Dracula.

The story revolves around Van Helsing being arrested for murdering Count Dracula while in the meantime Dracula's daughter, Countess Marya Zaleska goes about London town following in her father's footsteps causing a similar, bloody trail. Ironically, the movie would herald the end of the first series of Universal Monster pictures. The run had been spurred on by the original movie and was now ending with its late and protracted sequel. Publicly, Universal announced that a combination of pressures from home over censorship approvals and then British banning of a number of horror movies put pressure on the studio to focus on other genres and keep away from horror. In reality these pressures were persistent but were not as considerable as Universal made out. The real reason behind the restructuring was that a few weeks before Dracula's Daughter had wrapped Laemmle finally lost control of the company his family had started. Budgetary overruns from this picture and a number of others accounted for a company deficit of over a million dollars for 1935. Creditors who had heard the news quickly called in their debts, and before Laemmle could react the creditors took over control of the studio in 1936 and got rid of both Carl Laemmle Jnr. and his father, who was still the majority shareholder. The new owners, a combination of successful businessmen and banks, shied away from garish horror movies and instead focused the studio's attention on more wholesome entertainment such as westerns and musicals. It would be a good three years before the studio again considered any more horror pictures.

Dracula's Daughter would not go on to repeat the same box office success of its original movie, despite a last minute parachuting-in of Legosi to help market the film. Critics and commentators who enjoyed the more dynamic script and flawless pace of the film welcomed it with open arms (the pace was actually more akin to that of the Spanish version). Others commented on possible lesbian undertones and that despite the fact that the movie starts right where the original ends, the film apparently took place in the modern-day 1930s, replacing original director Browning's Victorian gothic splendor. Audiences enjoyed the flick, and receipts were solid, however this was not enough to persuade the new owners of Universal to make any more horror pictures for the near future.

"The Castle of Dracula now stood out against the red sky, and every stone of its broken battlements was articulated against the light of the setting sun."

Taken from Stoker's original Dracula.

Dracula returns

The problem with the undead is that unlike the living they always come back, and Dracula was no exception. The new owners took the reins at Universal Studios with an emphasis on more family wholesome entertainment, effectively turning their backs on the monsters that had propped the coffers up for many years. Like all good victims in their movies, turning their backs on these monsters was not a wise move. It was the late 1930s and a production of Dracula was once again touring to packed audiences. This happened to coincide with a double feature in LA of both Dracula and Frankenstein playing at select movie theaters. This double feature was soon an overnight sensation, selling more tickets than the regular new movies that had recently been released. Other theaters across the US quickly followed suit. Before long the current releases were sidelined at the cinemas with the classic monsters being played 21 hours a day every day; the police were even called to manage the crowds, such were the demands. These crowds were made worse when the unemployed Lugosi was employed directly by the theaters in LA to make appearances at select showings. "Come see the horror in the flesh!" exhorted the commercials of the time.

All of which was great for struggling Lugosi who had been striving to pay medical bills for his newborn son; struggles that led to him losing his large family home and having to downsize to a smaller apartment. Lugosi loved meeting the fans and the fans loved him. This renewed wave of interest was great for the actor and for the cinemas that were enjoying receipts. It was not, however, great news for Universal. They had rented the movies out to the theaters for a flat rate with little expectation. So when the monster craze of the late 1930s happened, they were not receiving the profits they should have been. But Universal didn't lose out for long; they quickly issued 500 new prints of the popular movies and started their own publicity campaign, effectively getting the movies back into cinemas right across the US. Lugosi was rehired and was sent out right across the Western seaboard, appearing at select theaters to drum up further business. This re-employment and boom in interest towards the franchise enabled Universal's now more settled owners to review their business models. It was quickly decided that like all good businesses, they should follow the money and get the monsters back into production as soon as possible. Lugosi and his young family were now out of their financial woes and he was again very much in demand. He said at the time:

"I owe it all to that little man at the Regina Theatre. I was dead, and he brought me back to life."

The Wilshire Regina Theatre as it looked at the time in Los Angeles

Other installments

Lugosi was back at work with all the regular main players at Universal making scores of new movies for their monster collection. He would not, however, be back for third installment in their Dracula franchise, that of Son of Dracula from 1943. Instead, Lon Chaney Jnr would don the famous cloak and fangs. Chaney, who by this time was a well- established actor for the studio (like his father before him), was cast into the central role of the vampire. The studio had initially thought to bring Lugosi into the picture (as after all he was on their books) but decided against it in an effort to promote the picture as the logical next stage of the classic franchise. Some loved the new edition, which was more akin to his environment as it was set in the new world. Others, however, pointed to the fact that he lacked the old-world imperialistic charm that Lugosi bellowed in spades. Whatever your inclination, the movie was a reasonable hit and helped keep the franchise alive and kicking. The movie is also notable for being the first time that special effects were used to change the vampire into a bat and vice versa; achieved using a combination of onscreen trickery and animation, the technique proved very popular with the paying audiences. The effect had been achieved by John P. Fulton who was the full time manager of the Special Effects Department at Universal and had previously won an Academy Award for his work on The Ten Commandments. Universal had brought him into their company to meet the ever-increasing demands from these movies to provide stylistic thrills to set them apart from the other studios.

After this movie, House of Frankenstein (1944) would star the famous Count but this time played comfortably by John Carradine, who would also play the character again in 1945 with House of Dracula. Carradine then went on to play the part three more times. House of Dracula had a working title of Dracula vs. the Wolf Man and was one of the first iterations to combine more than one of their popular franchises in one movie. It would be the 1948 movie Abbott and Costello Meet Frankenstein that would see Lugosi snatch the cape back from Carradine to play his most famous part once again. However, it was felt that by this time that the comedy-horror mash-up would be the swan song of the franchise, effectively ending the run of movies to feature the original classic monsters. This move would make way for newer and different custodians for the popular franchise; a move that was facilitated by a post-war world that was starting to look to a bright and modern future. Sci-fi influences would now have a heavier draw for audiences with the stuffy gothic monsters of the black and white era becoming a thing of the past. This movie would mark the last time that Lugosi played the infamous Count for Universal, though he would play the character or versions of the character elsewhere during his long career. He would also ride the wave of renewed interest in the popular movies of the 1950s, living long enough to become a beloved national icon before passing away quietly in his sleep in 1956. Contrary to varying accounts, it is true that Lugosi was buried in the full costume he so loved to wear. One funeral attendee was alleged to have said, "Should we drive a stake through his heart just to be sure?"

Dracula Untold (2014)

"My father was a great man, a hero, so they say. But sometimes the world doesn't need another hero, sometimes what it needs is a monster."

Director Gary Shore's feature film debut was Dracula Untold. It was quite a film to begin his career with, due to the ingenuity, excellent shoot quality and overall showing at the box office. In 2007, production of the movie began with Alex Proyas at the helm as director. Universal Studios tasked him with the film that at the time was titled Dracula: Year Zero; due to a change in budget, Universal passed on Proyas and tapped Gary Shore instead to direct the film. The star that was initially chosen was Sam Worthington. Worthington was a popular Australian actor who starred in such films as Macbeth and The Great Raid along with the Australia-based television series Love My Way.

The film's script was written by Burk Sharpless and Matt Sazama. The writing team worked together successfully after penning scripts for such hits as The Last Witch Hunter, Clue, and Flash Gordon. The film's producers and director chose to use Northern Ireland as the backdrop location. Along with Universal Studios, Legendary Pictures also supported the film financially. What made Sharpless and Sazama's story so unique was its direct connection between Vlad the Impaler from history and the character Dracula. Other stories drew influence from the historical character Vlad, but never directly stated that the two - Vlad and Dracula - are one in the same.

Sam Worthington took on the main role as Vlad the Impaler, but his involvement in the movie did not come to pass. Although contracts were confirmed, Worthington bowed out of the film and he was replaced in April of 2013 with Luke Evans. He had just starred in Furious 6 (for Universal) and prior to that No One Lives. He found a new challenge with Dracula because of the range of emotions and situations that the character goes through in the picture.

Playing alongside Evans, Sara Gadon was chosen as his wife, Zach McGowan was signed as gypsy Shkelgim, and Samantha Banks was chosen to portray the witch, although her character didn't make it to the film in editing. The role of Vlad's son was to be played by Art Parkinson.

What makes Dracula Untold different is its unique storyline of Vlad the Impaler being the Dracula character. Vlad starts off noble enough, living as the Prince of Transylvania. Though he is feared because of his former slaying of thousands and impaling them on spears, he now is content to live peacefully with the neighboring kingdoms. Of course this is Hollywood and his contentment can't last long. He soon is threatened by Mehmed II who demands 1,000 boys, including Vlad's son, for an army. Vlad tries to negotiate without sending his son off to fight, to no avail. This leads to Vlad making the decision to become a vampire and to tap into the supernatural powers that vampires possess.

Northern Ireland was the setting for the film. Initially it began in August of 2013. The following year in October, reshoots were scheduled. Part of the new goal was to get the movie ready to be included in Universal Studio's new monster cinematic universe. It was confirmed by the film's producer, Alissa Phillips, that this film would be included in the big-budget retelling of these horror characters. She also stated that it was hoped that Vlad from the movie would make a cameo appearance in the forthcoming The Mummy, which is a Tom Cruise version of the epic tale that is currently in production. Director Gary Shore stated that it was intentionally filmed to allow the studio to use it if they chose as a launching pad for future films in a series.

The film was captivating for its storytelling, but also for its cinematic quality. Music was a big part of its delivery, including a premiere music score composed by Ramin Djawadi. Djawadi was known at the time for his Iron Man score that earned him a Grammy nomination.

The Dracula Untold release date was altered four times. Initially it was scheduled to make its debut on August 8, 2014. It was pushed to October 3rd and then to October the 17th. Finally, October 10th was the target date, with producers stating that releasing it on this date would give it three-weeks' worth of runtime before Halloween. They believed that timing would be essential to the movie's success, and capitalizing on Halloween was critical.

The film was released in North America on the date three weeks prior to Halloween as finally announced. It earned just shy of $9m on the opening day and made it to the number two slot on the box office that weekend. It was right behind the mega-hit Gone Girl in the standings. The film made it to a slew of IMAX theaters. In the end, it brought in a worldwide total of just over $215,500,000 and had a budget of just over $70m. By all accounts it was a successful movie.

Dracula Untold: Reign of Blood was announced in early August of 2014 as house for Orlando and Hollywood's upcoming respective Halloween Horror Nights event. Based on the movie on the same name, the house would act as an "immersive preview" for guests that would take them into the heart of the movie with key scenes like the destroyed village and a network of caves before ending at the vampire's castle (which was a very similar route to the event that The Wolfman had done in 2009). Whereas the film focused on the origins of Dracula, the house would focus on the horrors he perpetrated, as John Murdy, creative director of the Hollywood Horror Nights, where the house would also debut, explained:

"But there is much more to the tale than just a dark figure lurking in the shadows, drinking blood. While Dracula Untold will reveal the origin story of the man who became Dracula, our Halloween Horror Nights maze will invite guests to experience the atrocities Dracula imposed on his victims in the most frightening and immersive way possible."

That year it was found that Hollywood's version of this house was by far the superior to Orlando's. Hollywood used far more detailed and immersive sets to heighten the tension and suspense within the house. Orlando chose to undertake more of a retelling of the story, showing that the character was slowly morphing into a supernatural being in order to defeat his enemies.

FRANKENSTEIN'S
MONSTER

"It was on a dreary night of November that I beheld the accomplishment of my toils. With an anxiety that almost amounted to agony, I collected the instruments of life around me, that I might infuse a spark of being into the lifeless thing that lay at my feet. It was already one in the morning; the rain pattered dismally against the panes, and my candle was nearly burnt out, when, by the glimmer of the half-extinguished light, I saw the dull yellow eye of the creature open..."

Revolutionary roots

From around the end of the seventeenth century right through to the early nineteenth century, Western Europe went through a cultural change that affected a whole manner of aspects, including but not limited to: philosophy, politics, communications, medicine, art and science, with the latter of these having the largest bearing on our story. The period would be known as The Age of Enlightenment, and it would see technology and science rapidly grow and develop. Thinkers across the continent questioned everything they had been taught in order to bring clarity and to revolutionize the way in which people lived their lives. This process challenged the status quo, challenged authority, questioned religion, and brought rational thinking to a great a number of areas. Prior to this period, the ability to question the monarchy, the government or the church were out of the question, though the period was not without its conflict due to this step change. The period would ultimately produce a great number of essays, novels, periodicals, laws, books, scientific discoveries, wars, medical treatments, new factions of various religions, and revolts. This last was evident in the War of Independence that ultimately led to the setup of the United States of America itself and in the French Revolution too. Once the period was over it led into an era known as the Romantic Period or the Romantic Era, which is important to note as Frankenstein was a product of both periods. The former period would be as important to its development as it would become to the period that followed.

The Romantic Period originated in Europe in the later part of the eighteenth century and reached America at approximately the same time. Officially it is categorized as the period from 1800 through 1850. The term "Romanticism" may mislead some readers into thinking this was a romantic period, in the modern sense of romance as "love between partners." There was a "love" aspect to the period, but it is not the same as Romanticism in this sense.

Romanticism was a term that cited the artistic and literary movement of the world and focused on the individualism, intense emotion and heightened descriptions of the characters. For example, some popular artists of the time were Herman Melville and Edgar Allen Poe. Each one played well to the Romantic Period because of their realistic but dark characters who were rich with details. The most common character of the American version of Romanticism were alienated and almost haunting individuals who were isolated due to their darkness. They also were categorized by an ill fate that would most likely lead to anguish of spirit and possibly death in the end.

The reason for this delving into the darkness of human spirit was partially attributed to the condition of the world. Writers like Charles Dickens, for example, wrote about traditional familial communities and their struggles because this is what they experienced first-hand. American writers at this time of history were candid about their situations. It was the time of the Industrial Revolution, and that was reflected in various artistic works. American writers were sharing fiction where their characters lacked the traditional community values and organization. This was because at the time Americans were still gaining a footing in society and building the rules.

American novelists were in the unique position of relying on their own imaginations to conjure up definite cities and organized civilizations. The frontier was rife with immigrants who spoke different languages. They had varying ways of everyday life and formed a melting pot of defining daily lives. Because of this, most main characters who made it into American literature throughout the Romantic Period may have found themselves traveling alone, or experiencing feelings of loneliness and visions to follow. Melville's Typee saw the hero find himself maneuvering among cannibalistic tribes. Poe brought individuals who were almost always lonely figures to literature. Throughout the Romantic Period, novelists were forced to invent new forms of society and structure because they weren't there for them to report yet.

The Romantic Period was dark. It was a reflection of society's lack of stability and overall harrowing struggle that, more than likely, would end in either death or tragic disappointment. One example is Mellville's Moby-Dick, a novel in which only one character, Ishmael, survives. Another popular example is the death of Reverend Dimmesdale in The Scarlet Letter, who also dies in the end. These two characters are indicative of what the writing during this period was like. It was dark. It was intense. It was a literary method that brought about new techniques to create stories of fiction.

One of the main ideas that was bandied around throughout this time was the notion of humankind being "rational." The great thinkers of the time perpetuated the theory and following practice that man was capable of his/her own intelligence and thought enough to modify and undertake his/her own life. Many ran with this idea in an effort to show how authority in its negative connotation and the superiority of the Church should be questioned; which led to people wanting to make their own way in life without pain or punishment from an overbearing upper class. The times produced an upsurge of people who would call themselves Deists or agnostics, a great number of whom included the Founding Fathers.

Frankenstein, or to give the book its original title: Frankenstein; or, The Modern Prometheus was a novel written by the English author Mary Wollstonecraft Shelley, simply known to most as Mary Shelley. Her most well-known work was conceived and produced on a vacation, no less. Her husband Percy Shelley along with their young son travelled to Geneva with a mutual friend Claire Clairmont (the latest squeeze of the venerable Lord Byron, who they planned to meet once there). The group arrived in Geneva in May 1816. Byron, who had been delayed elsewhere, eventually arrived at their lodgings just over a week later. Byron did not travel alone and brought with him his friend and physician John William Polidori. Once together Byron rented a large villa close to Lake Geneva in the village of Cologny, whereas the Shelley family rented a waterfront property nearby. The vacation was spent writing, boating, walking, cooking, fishing, drinking, and talking long into the night.

Chillon Castle on the banks of Lake Geneva would have inspired Shelley

Unfortunately for both parties, the weather was poor and they spent more time inside due to the heavy rainfall, than outdoors. The party mostly congregated in Byron's larger villa where a large log fire and tales of mystery, intrigue, murder and ghosts were told, especially by Byron, who was quite the raconteur. One night after entertaining everyone for some hours, he proposed that as the weather was starting to use up his vast knowledge of European ghost stories, the whole party should retire to their quarters and return in the morning with their own ghost stories, that they were to each write themselves that night. Mary was unable to think of a story for the next day and was goaded by Byron every day after as she was unable to formalize something ghastly enough to satisfy the eager group whose tales were growing ever more horrific by each day. The vacation was not a short one, and Mary found that between the constant downpours she started to put together a suitably heinous story that would satisfy the party. It was mid-June on a now characteristically damp evening that inspiration struck; she imagined what would it be like and what would happen if someone who was dead could be physically brought back to life. That night the group retired around midnight, and unable to sleep due to the ideas racing round her head she began to write into the night, finishing sometime in the early hours of the morning. Her ghost story would literally be that of the actual 'walking dead,' she reportedly told the group at the time.

The next day she was back at it, scribbling away at a desk within the bedchambers. Initially, she believed the story to be a mere short story, but with encouragement from Percy she enlarged the story to become her very first novel. When the group returned to England she kept working on the book around her own duties until, some two years later in 1818, it was finished. It was first published anonymously in the same year; it would not be until the second edition of 1823 that her name was officially attached to the work. It was in this edition that Mary thanked her husband Percy for his help with creating the book, with a short notice at the start:

> *"I certainly did not owe the suggestion of one incident,*
> *nor scarcely of one train of feeling, to my husband, and*
> *yet but for his incitement, it would never have taken the*
> *form in which it was presented to the world."*

Frankenstein the novel would infuse elements from the populist gothic novels of their day along with notions from the emerging Romantic movement. And despite Shelley being asked to create a ghost story for her vacation, and the fact that most people consider the book to be that of horror, it can be considered that her novel is one of the very first iterations of science-fiction, a genre of fiction that was in its infancy during this time.

Shelley later remarked that inspiration came from her former travels around Europe some years prior. She travelled along a course that would eventually follow the River Rhine in Germany. It was likely here that she first saw the name "Frankenstein" as is here on the banks of this river at Gernsheim that Castle Frankenstein is located. It was supposedly home to an alchemist, which was a popular pastime for many would-be scientists before and during the Enlightenment. Mentally noting the wicked and wonderful experiments that the alchemist must have undertaken in order to produce gold must have had an impact on the fledgling writer at the time. It was hearty mixture of the tales of the occult and the dead walking the earth combined with these earlier vacations that must have spun into the story we know today. Shelley would also recount many years later:

> *"When I was about fifteen years old we had retired to our*
> *house near Belrive, when we witnessed a most violent and*
> *terrible thunderstorm. Before this I was not unacquainted*

with the more obvious laws of electricity. On this occasion a man of great research in natural philosophy was with us, and, excited by this catastrophe, he entered on the explanation of a theory which he had formed on the subject of electricity and galvanism, which was at once new and astonishing to me. All that he said threw greatly into the shade Cornelius Agrippa, Albertus Magnus, and Paracelsus, the lords of my imagination."

The story gave us the young, enigmatic Dr. Victor Frankenstein who is dedicated to the scientific world through experimentation and discovery. Through his work he enthused about discovering the new and never-before seen. This dedication leads him to experiment with reanimation, and through this process he becomes the embodiment of the Enlightenment as he acts without morals or the influence of a higher power's statement of ethics. Instead, the sheer ambition to discover and create the new pushes the plucky protagonist to create the monster we all know. The monster of the book is a curious creature that wants to desperately understand the world around him; he seeks to expand his knowledge and learn right from wrong, a process that he undertakes from knowing the difference between pleasure and pain, a process that enables the monster to look on and understand the world without invested knowledge of a parent or teachings from Christ.

"But where were my friends and relations? No father had watched my infant days, no mother had blessed me with smiles and caresses; or if they had, all my past life was now a blot, a blind vacancy in which I distinguished nothing. From my earliest remembrance I had been as I then was in height and proportion. I had never yet seen a being resembling me or who claimed any intercourse with me. What was I? The question again recurred, to be answered only with groans.

I will soon explain to what these feelings tended, but allow

*me now to return to the cottagers, whose story excited in
me such various feelings of indignation, delight, and
wonder, but which all terminated in additional love and
reverence for my protectors (for so I loved, in an innocent,
half-painful self-deceit, to call them)."*

It was much later in 1831 that the first definitive edition of the
novel we know now was published in London by Colburn and
Bentley. Shelley had heavily revised this edition. A more
confident writer by this time, she sought to make the work more
complete and bowed to few pressures to tidy sections that she
need not alter. It became a longer version of the original and
contained a new preface which established a version of how the
book was first put together (though it was not factually correct).
This edition also establishes once and for all that Mary, not Percy
Shelley, was in fact the original author, though Percy did aid in the
production by giving his new author and wife a great number of
pointers. The need to definitively define who the author was
became a driving motive for this and the former edition. One of
the largest criticisms of the original release was that no one took
ownership of the text, which confused both readers and critics
alike. Shelley had been schooled at a young age, a luxury that
was not afforded to all people, let alone women, during these
days. Her schooling, combined with her father's connections,
ensured that growing up she was aware of experimentation on
corpses and the new science of electricity. It would be this made-
up blend of theories in the novel that critics argued was hogwash,
which it was, but Shelley was not presenting the book as scientific
fact but indeed a stretch of the imagination presented in a gothic
context. The other main point that most critics did not like about
the work was the book's handling of morality and ethics,
particularly regarding the relationship that exists between all living
things and God.

"I thought I saw Elizabeth, in the bloom of health, walking

*in the streets of Ingolstadt. Delighted and surprised, I
embraced her, but as I imprinted the first kiss on her lips,
they became livid with the hue of death; her features
appeared to change, and I thought that I held the corpse
of my dead mother in my arms; a shroud enveloped her
form, and I saw the grave-worms crawling in the folds of
the flannel. I started from my sleep with horror; a cold
dew covered my forehead, my teeth chattered, and every
limb became convulsed; when, by the dim and yellow
light of the moon, as it forced its way through the window
shutters, I beheld the wretch - the miserable monster
whom I had created."*

Formerly known as Royal Coburg Theatre, The Old Vic in London held the

first performance of this chilling tale

Despite the lukewarm reception from the critics, the book did prove to be a commercial success with readers swamping bookshops across the Continent to get their copy of this work. By 1823 the book had become such a sellout success that a play entitled Resumption; or The Fate of Frankenstein appeared in London by Richard Brinsley Peake. In 1826 the famous playwright Henry M. Milner presented his own play adaptation, The Man and The Monster; or The Fate of Frankenstein which opened on 3rd July at the Royal Coburg Theatre in London. Shelley was rumored to have attended both versions of her most famous work. The plays intensified public interest in the novel and would ensure constant reprints were forthcoming during these years, despite the critics' reactions. Many suspected that the male-dominated literary critics were more angry that the unknown author of the original work turned out to be a woman; whatever the reason, the public did not care as they loved the gothic novel and all of the stage plays.

The first feature films of Frankenstein

The very first film adaptation of the play came in 1910 when Edison Studios produced Frankenstein. J. Searle Dawley would direct it with Charles Stanton Ogle as the haphazard monster. Edison Studios had become a subsidiary of the Edison Manufacturing Company, a company founded in 1889 by the inventor Thomas Edison to manufacture, amongst many ideas, the first batteries and electrical equipment. It began to showcase its many products, including the camera, by producing a number of short movies based on very famous properties.

The director, who was an engineer by day, shot the movie over a total of just three days during the summer of 1910 in the back streets of the Bronx, New York, and although Edison had little to do with the production, he worked as producer of the work. In order to not cause too much offense (it was, after all 1910), the horror and gothic elements were toned down with a heightened emphasis on the mystic and psychological woes that the monster would face in "modern" New York.

The Edison Studios version of the chilling tale

Though little is known about the film, it was actually lost for many decades before being found in 1963. The only hint that it had existed was the mention of the piece within old Edison Company brochures. It was subsequently restored and protected for prosperity, making it the first official version of the infamous tale.

Although this Edison version was lost and then found some time later, the next edition of Frankenstein was not so lucky. Life Without Soul would be released just five years later in 1915 by Ocean Pictures. Perhaps for the time, it could be considered Frankenstein's first big screen debut, though no surviving prints of the film exist so no one is sure exactly how the monster looked.

The film's plot also diverts heavily from the original work with one critic stating that it is "reminiscent" of the original piece. The story largely focuses on a doctor who creates his own man, in his image though completely soulless. The English-born actor Percy Darrell played the monster or, as he was known in this iteration, "the Brute Man." Playing to the gothic roots of the original, the movie is very much a horror story where the Brute murders his creator's sister on her wedding night. The movie then ensues into a caper across the European continent with the Doctor attempting to kill his creation before he murders again. The story wraps up with the notion that the film was just a horrible dream by a young man who had read the original novel and had fallen asleep afterwards. The film would be reissued a year later with added scientific documentary footage detailing the reproduction methods of fish; this was the last time this movie was seen in public. Yet despite one further outing in the Italian silent picture The Monster of Frankenstein in 1920, the monster would not be seen again on the big screen until the advent of sound, where undoubtedly the most recognized version of the tale is told.

Frankenstein (1931)

> "How do you do? Mr. Carl Laemmle feels it would be a little unkind to present this picture without just a friendly word of warning: We are about to unfold the story of Frankenstein, a man of science who sought to create a man after his own image without reckoning upon God. It is one of the strangest tales ever told. It deals with the two great mysteries of creation: life and death. I think it will thrill you. It may shock you. It might even horrify you. So, if any of you feel that you do not care to subject your nerves to such a strain, now's your chance to uh, well, – we warned you!"

James Whale director of Universal's Frankenstein

Dracula had been a rip-roaring success for Universal who at the time had been suffering from poor box-office receipts for the past few years. It was on the news of this movie's success that very day that Carl Laemmle Jr. immediately held a production meeting to get another "monster" picture into production as soon as possible. Following various production meetings, it was agreed that Universal's next monster picture should be Frankenstein. Lugosi, who during these months, was riding the wave of interest in his new-found fame initially assumed he would play the title role of the doctor, however he would first be offered the role of the Monster instead. Accepting the challenge, Lugosi sat down with the makeup team at the studio and undertook a number of makeup tests to see how they could transform the actor into the horrific creature. It didn't go well. The tests made the actor resemble more of a goblin-like fiend rather than a monster made of dead body parts. Scripts revisions were also prevalent during these weeks and eventually Lugosi left the production to work on other projects. The final straw for the actor came when the last rewrite he saw had the monster as a relentless killing machine with no remorse or emotion. Lugosi reportedly remarked, "I was a star in my country and I will not be a scarecrow over here!" Others commentated that it was not the script that pushed the Dracula star out the door but the initial assumption from the actor who had refilled the Universal coffers that he should be offered the title role and not the unidentifiable mute killing machine. Whatever the reason, the director Robert Florey was also detached from the project when Universal replaced him with English director James Whale. It is likely that Whale may have made the call to replace Lugosi if he had shown little interest in the character.

James Whale, who had made his name making these new talkie pictures, was regarded as hot property in the early 1930s. Any director who transitioned from silent to sound in a commercial and artistically successful way was working hard within the studio system at a time of great upheaval for the industry at large; Whale was one of the directors who was attracting great attention from the studios. He was snapped up by Laemmle in 1931 and signed a five-year contract to work on a large number of movies within the studio, the first being Waterloo Bridge which was released that same year. The movie garnered much critical praise and became a favorite that year of the studio bosses; so much so that the company then offered Whale a golden opportunity – the ability to openly chose to work on any movie that the studio had agreed to produce. The list was not as inspiring as Whale had immediately hoped; the list was mostly war dramas or cowboy movies, except one, that of Frankenstein. Despite the picture already being a developed production, the director and leading man (as we have seen) were both moved to make way for Whale. Not wanting to lose their talented staffers, Florey and Lugosi actually ended up being moved to another picture that went into production some weeks later entitled The Murders in the Rue Morgue, a picture inspired by the famous work of Edgar Allen Poe. Lugosi would play the monster one day, but not on this occasion.

The original script called for many changes from the original Shelley source material. Instead, the writers would focus their efforts on emulating the scripts of the great stage versions of the famous tale. The original text uses the point of view of both Dr. Frankenstein and that of Captain Walton. The scriptwriters, as in the play versions, removed Walton to give the narrative a more filmic flow without the disjointed nature of switching between points of view. The next most notable change would be that of the Monster. In the novel the creature is more humane, whereas in the script they called for him to be more dehumanized. The creature would become sub-human and barely capable of individual thought or reflection, often using violence to replace any feelings of sorrow. The Monster was not without sympathy or pathos, as shown in the sequence where he kills the little girl. This changed from the original where he saves the girl, to a version where he kills her but does not understand what he has done. Together these sequences were added to the script to try and add some spark of humanity to the creature, despite him having the stolen "abnormal brain."

> "There's nothing to fear. Look. No blood, no decay. Just a few stitches. And look, here's the final touch.
> (Frankenstein uncovers a bandaged and wrapped head.)
> The brain you stole, Fritz. (He shows Fritz that he has installed the brain that was stolen from the medical school.) Think of it. The brain of a dead man waiting to live again in a body I made with my own hands, with my own hands. Let's have one final test. Throw the switches."

There were a great many other alterations to the script from the original novel, mostly added by Whale. Victor Frankenstein became Henry Frankenstein, his friend Clerval would become Victor and the connection of Elizabeth being his cousin was also removed. Other than these relationship and name changes, the Doctor is fairly presented as similar to the original story, apart from his ending. In this script he would survive and has a happy ending, whereas in the novel he was not so lucky.

Whale took up the gothic monster picture with great enthusiasm. He totally revised the script as above, he moved the art direction on to incorporate more lavishly appointed sets and started to spend up his budget. Management became quickly concerned over the actions of the flamboyant Englishman. Fears were suppressed some weeks later when principal photography began and Universal executives could see where their dollars had been spent. Kenneth Strickfaden had been appointed by Whale to design unique and spellbinding electrical effects to be used within the scene where the Monster is brought to life. This iconic use of lighting and technology would then be synonymous with all future Universal-made incarnations of the famous tale.

Bulbs, test tubes, burners, circuitry, and even a Tesla Coil or two from the actual inventor Nikola Tesla were all procured to create this unique scene from within the movie. Strickfaden also doubled for Karloff in a number of short sequences during the filming of this sequence. Karloff was concerned that he may get burned from the sparks the setup gave out. Though Karloff did receive some minor burns from molten metal pouring off of one of the lamps, the scene did proceed exactly as both Strickfaden and Whale had planned. That was until one of the very final lines of the sequence was cut in post-production:

> *"It's alive! It's alive! In the name of God! Now I know what it feels like to be God!"*

This line was shouted in total ecstasy when the Doctor realizes that he has brought life to the monster. Whale considered the line to be integral to the emotion of the sequence. However, many state censors did not agree and found the line to be wholly blasphemous. It was later cut, despite Whale's severe objections to the eventual compromise: just "It's alive! It's alive!", followed by a crudely-added addition of a loud lightning bolt which cuts out the rest of his words. It wasn't until many decades later, on home release, that the line was restored and is still part of the film now.

The role of the Monster following Lugosi's departure would be offered to the little-known English immigrant actor William Henry Pratt or, to use his recently-adopted stage name, Boris Karloff. He met with Universal's makeup authority Jack Pierce and they discussed the role and the need for the Monster to have the ability to convey a sense of pathos through the grease paint and prosthetics, as Whale wished. Karloff said:

> "I had no idea the importance of the role, but Jack Pierce did: he stalled the test two weeks while working on makeup, and the makeup sold the part."

It would be a combination of Karloff's expert acting ability and Pierce's aptitude to create a monster that leads us to fear yet feel sympathy for one of the most iconic motion picture creatures of all time. Pierce would recall many years later:

> "I did not depend on imagination. In 1931, before I did a bit of designing, I spent three months of research in anatomy, surgery, medicine, criminal history, criminology, ancient and modern burial customs, and electrodynamics. My anatomical studies taught me that there are six ways a surgeon can cut the skull in order to take out or put in a brain. I figured that Frankenstein, who was a scientist but no practicing surgeon, would take the simplest surgical way. He would cut the top of the skull off straight across

like a potlid, hinge it, pop the brain in and then clamp it on tight. That is the reason I decided to make the Monster's head square and flat like a shoe box and dig that big scar across his forehead with the metal clamps holding it together."

The director, James Whale, summed up how the audience had reacted to Karloff's makeup and performance:

"I consider the creation of the Monster to be the high spot of the film, because if the audience did not believe the thing had been really made, they would not be bothered with what it was supposed to afterward. By this time, the audience must at least believe something is going to happen. It might be disaster, but at least they'll settle down to see the show."

Pierce made fake head clasps that wrapped around the actor's head with a square top, he applied fake skin and packing to blend it in seamlessly. He fixed wire clamps over Karloff's lips (he even had a dentist remove several molars) and painted his skin green with a hint of blue which under the heavy lights of the set would make his skin appear to be gray in coloration, like that of a corpse. Karloff was instrumental in the design for the "dead eyes" that the character had. It was a combination of waxing his eyelids and applying subtle color and putty effects to make his eyes look wild and confused at the world around him. The suit he wore was designed to be undersized and ill-fitting to make his limbs appear to be bigger than they were. This was topped-off with extremely heavy boots on platform heels to give him the characteristic, shuffling walk we now appreciate from this character. The process

was grueling, with the actor sitting in the chair for hours. Karloff
would say of experience:

> "I spent three-and-a-half hours in the make-up chair
> getting ready for the day's work. The make-up itself was
> quite painful, particularly the putty on my eyes. There
> were days when I thought I would never be able to hold
> out until the end of the day."

Principle photography was undertaken in the summer of 1931
utilizing both soundstages and the vast Universal Studios backlot.
The Little Europe sets which had been built years earlier, including
the Court of Miracles (complete with fiberglass fountain), were
used as the village of Goldstadt; particular scenes of note for these
sets were the wedding of Henry Frankenstein in the square and the
reveal of the murder of the little girl. Contrary to popular belief,
the lake where the murder takes place was not shot on the backlot,
it was filmed some 30 miles away at Malibou Lake near the Santa
Monica Mountains by Agoura Hills, California. All the other
scenes in the movie were shot in soundstages back at Universal
City. Frankenstein's laboratory was constructed on Stage 12,
which was one of a number of new soundstages built to house the
new talkie movies in 1929. All of the sets were built from timber
with a number of backcloths thrown around to create size and
atmosphere. Unfortunately, the producers of the movie had not
accounted for the need to add additional Foley to the picture, that
is why a number of scenes sound very basic as the actors' feet
walking on timber boards(instead of what should be stone) is
clearly audible.

The Court of Miracles located on the Universal Studios' backlot was used for many of the locations in Frankenstein. It would later be used for countless entries from the Universal Monster's catalogue. It is still standing and is used repeatedly for many productions to this day.

The efforts of all were not undertaken in vain. The movie would open on November 4th 1931 at the Mayfair Theater in New York's Time Square and like its vampiric predecessor, the movie would be an instant hit. It played to packed movie houses, it was awarded the New York Times' Movie of the Year Award, and earned Universal a cool $12m; a pill which softened the initial blow of Whales' over expenditure on the picture (the final budget was just shy of $260,000 dollars). This movie, along with Dracula, had now elevated the fledgling movie studio from a small contributor in the industry to a major movie production powerhouse.

Boris Karloff the little known British actor would grow to become a mainstay for the Universal Monster movie franchise.

Although the cast, crew and studio were very happy, the movie would see some revision from the persistent censors. As mentioned, the infamous God line was removed early on, and also on the editor's room floor was the sequence where the Monster meets a little girl by the lake. Many statewide and international censors took exception to the scene, with most demanding it be removed (despite the fact that the scene is quite crucial for the movie's story). Likewise, the scene with Fritz's hanged body, the murder of Dr. Waldmann, and some of the final sequence were all requested on a state-by-state basis. Whale remonstrated that by the time the movie had been cut and recut by the overly zealous censors there would not be much of the movie left to see. However, despite the censors' demands the movie would be a massive hit, terrifying audiences across the world.

The Bride of Frankenstein

> "Dr. Frankenstein: [after seeing Pretorius' creations] But this isn't science. It's more like black magic.
>
> Dr. Pretorius: You think I'm mad. Perhaps I am. But listen, Henry Frankenstein. While you were digging in your graves, piecing together dead tissues, I, my dear pupil, went for my material to the source of life. I grew my creatures, like cultures, grew them as nature does, from seed."

It was four years later in 1935, following the success of the first picture, that Universal finally released the highly-anticipated sequel to their original Frankenstein movie. Most of the original cast and crew returned for the sequel, including leading man Colin Clive as Henry Frankenstein, Karloff as the monster, and director James Whale. In addition to these, a new star, Elsa Lanchester, was cast as the bride.

As with the earlier Dracula sequel, the movie begins right where the original finished. Largely working to a subplot from the original text, the movie shows reformed character Henry

Frankenstein abandoning his plans to create life within his laboratory and creating a new life for himself with his bride. Unfortunately, he is threatened by the Monster and then coerced by his old mentor Dr. Pretorius to return to work to aid him in constructing a mate for the Monster.

The movie was planned soon after the massive box-office returns had been received by Universal. Senior management were quick to green-light the sequel and get it into theaters as soon as possible. Owing to the fact that the original ending of the first movie was changed to a 'happy ending' (mostly due to pressures from the Censors) this good fortune meant that they could afford the sequel to commence right after the action of the original. Initially Whale was not keen to return and was allegedly reported as saying that he had "squeezed the idea dry" and so would not return for more. His success with other Universal properties (including The Invisible Man) ensured that in the eyes of Carl Laemmle Jr. there could be no other man fill the director's shoes for this sequel. Whale, taking advantage of his recent success, agreed a deal with the company and he was soon appointed to the role.

The first script that was submitted by returning writer Robert Florey was entitled The New Adventures of Frankenstein - The Monster Lives! The script focused on a Monster that had been left abandoned and struggling to understand the world around him. The script was subsequently rejected without comment from Universal, which pushed the project back a whole year. Next up, Universal staff writer Tom Reed wrote a new treatment entitled The Return of Frankenstein which was far more in the vein of the original movie. Universal accepted the new script, feeling it was a happy medium, containing something new but retaining all the classical elements of the first picture. It did however have one problem: Whale hated it. He dragged his heels but took the bold move to scrap the script (despite the months of pre-production and storyboarding that had been undertaken) and released Reed from the production. The next writers that were assigned were L. G. Blochman and Philip MacDonald. They collaborated to produce a script that was set more in a modern setting with the Monster at large in the modern world. Again, Whale on receiving the final copy found it wholly unsatisfactory and again released this duo of writers to work elsewhere. Whale was starting to annoy the Universal bosses who did not like this constant reshuffling of the writing staff within the picture. The movie had now been in production for over three years and was starting to be the "turkey" of their upcoming attractions.

By 1934 Whale had drafted in a new writer, John L. Balderston, to work on yet another version of the script, this time working more closely with Whale. Balderston happened on an idea based on an original theme in the novel – the Monster's demands for a mate. Within the original novel, the Monster is to receive a mate built much in the way he was created, but after reflection by Frankenstein the mate is destroyed before it is brought to life. Balderston thought that this would be the perfect means upon which to hinge the entire movie. Unfortunately, Balderston and Whale would eventually fall out, with Whale complaining that Balderston had great ideas but that they were not being developed in the manner that Whale wanted. For a record at the time, Whale took the unprecedented steps to again fire his chief writer and instead appoint William J. Hurlbut and Edmund Pearson, who came from more theatrical backgrounds. They would work on the script left by Balderston combining most of his ideas and some of his theatrical elements to create the script that was finally shot in 1935, some four years later than planned.

Again, longtime Universal player Bela Lugosi was considered for the role of Frankenstein's mentor, Dr. Pretorius. It was also rumored to have been offered to Claude Rains fresh from his success in The Invisible Man. Instead it would be offered to Ernest Thesiger. Elizabeth, Henry Frankenstein's lover was replaced at the last hour by Valerie Hobson, following an illness that kept Mae

Clarke from working at the time. Nearly all the other cast and crew members returned to their roles to shoot the picture.

The Bride amongst the other characters onset

Whale, whilst auditioning actresses for the title role as the Bride, decided upon the notion that the actress he would offer the part to should be comfortable about undertaking two roles within the picture, that of the Bride and also Mary Shelley. A remnant left over from one of the early drafts of the script saw the original author of the novel giving a prologue about the movie. Whale revived this notion as he wanted to show how this horrific story had sprung from the imagination of an average but beautiful young woman – in part to honor his fellow countrywomen; it would also be a countrywoman who would ultimately be offered the part. Initially considering Brigitte Helm and Phyllis Brook, he eventually decided to offer the role to little-known English actress Elsa Lanchester, who was married to the renowned stage and screen actor Charles Laughton. Laughton was an acquaintance of Whale's and they had worked together previously. Lanchester, who had found it difficult to work in Hollywood, had only done so to accompany her husband there for his career. Having limited success, she returned to England to their home in London, and on the very day of her return she was contacted by Whale who offered her the two parts. She accepted and rejoined her husband in Hollywood to take up the roles.

Colin Clive also returned to play the title role within the picture. Initially, Universal were not keen on his return. It was rumored that Clive's battle with alcoholism was starting to consume the actor. He was rumored to have been erratic on other pictures and rather than risking the appointment of an unreliable actor to the title role, Universal asked Whale recast the role. Whale refused and said the picture would be dead without the unmistakable excellence of his leading man. In fact, some sources say that Clive's more hysterical portrayal of the character within the film is due to his private battle with alcohol, though this is unsubstantiated.

Karloff was also back and had been involved with some of the later script development. A late entry into the dynamic of the script's development was the ability of the Monster to speak. Karloff was reported as saying:

> "Speech? Stupid! My argument was that if the monster had any impact or charm, it was because he was inarticulate; this great, lumbering, inarticulate creature. The moment he spoke you might as well ... play it straight."

The need for the Monster to speak would also alter the look of the creature as in order for Karloff to utter the new lines he would have to remove his dental plate which gave him his characteristic gaunt look in the original. It was decided that he would have learnt a basic repertoire of 45 simple words that he could use to converse within the movie; the arbitrary number was decided upon based on the recommendation of the studio's onsite psychiatrist. In the original movie, Karloff had been credited as "?" whereas in the sequel he would be credited simply as "Karloff" (a trait that Universal would follow for a number of his roles). Elsa Lanchester would be billed first as Mary Wollstonecraft Shelley for her prologue and then as "?," in a tribute to Karloff's entry in the original movie.

"What a setting in that churchyard to begin with. The sobbing women, the first plod of earth on the coffin. That was a pretty chill. Frankenstein and the dwarf stealing the body out of its new-made grave, cutting the hanged man down from the gallows where he swung creaking in the wind. The cunning of Frankenstein in his mountain laboratory, picking dead men apart and building up a human Monster, so fearful - so horrible that only a half-crazed brain could have devised. And then the murder! The little child drowned. Henry Frankenstein himself thrown from the top of the burning mill by the very Monster he had created. And it was these fragile white fingers that penned the nightmare."

Jack Pierce was also back and again, like the original design of the Monster, he would also look to create another unmistakable and wholly inhuman design for the Bride. Working closely with Whale it was decided early on that her hair and the style of it should be the main focal point of her appearance. Taking inspiration from ancient Egyptian designs the pair decided upon having it put up in a Marcel wave style but woven into a wire frame to heighten the appearance of this otherworldly being. Lanchester disliked sitting for hours at a time in the makeup chair with Pierce working around her, and they reportedly fell out during production. Lanchester recalled years later:

> "...really did feel that he made these people, like he was a god ... in the morning he'd be dressed in white as if he were in hospital to perform an operation."

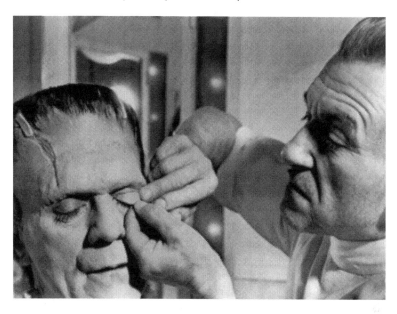

Makeup artist Jack Pierce would work on scores of Universal pictures starting off with The Man Who Laughs in 1928

For her role as Shelley, she wore a large period-type dress that was embroidered with sequins and highly appointed to show respect to the original author. It was reported that the dress took 17 women over 12 weeks to make to the satisfaction of Whale.

Whilst Pierce worked on Lanchester, he also worked on Karloff to update the look of the Monster from the original. Both Pierce and Whale wanted special consideration given to the look of the

Monster owing to the fact that he would now be speaking within the film and would therefore have more screen time. They looked at the significant events from the first picture, noting the fire and the knocks he received. They decided to add this patina to his appearance, adding in some mild singe marks and scars whilst shortening his hair to show some distress. Pierce also worked a great deal on set to ensure the wounds he had added were starting to "heal" throughout the piece. Both Karloff and Whale were very pleased with Pierce's attention to detail throughout the production.

Kenneth Strickfaden also returned for the sequel. He ensured after the completion of the original movie that all the original set pieces, including all the laboratory he had meticulously assembled, were retained and protected for future use. He recycled a great many items for use within the picture. He would also work closely with John P. Fulton, who by this time was head of special effects at Universal. The pair created the sequences involving the "baby monster" and the lightning effects (the latter of which would be used in stock footage and reused hundreds of times for many Universal movies and TV shows).

Franz Waxman scored the movie. He worked with Whale to create three distinctive themes, one for each of the Monster, the Bride, and Dr. Pretorius. Taking cues from the original, he created a unique and haunting soundtrack that helped elevate the picture past the usual shock and awe scores of some of the other monster movies being made at the time. He also took heavy direction from Whale who devised a plan to have the final melody of the movie be as discordant as the action on screen so that the audience would believe that the theater they were in was being affected by the movie. This was an early example of the brilliant director attempting to utilize sound to really emote the audience throughout the picture, a technique that was innovative at the time.

Principal photography began on January 2nd 1935 with a budget of $290,000, which was similar to the budget of the original. The shoot for the picture was around eight weeks in length with most of the action taking place on the backlot at Universal. Despite the years of planning, the shoot featured a great many setbacks. It is likely that Universal was angry at Whale's delays as he fired the series of writing staffers and that filming was accelerated to bring the picture into theaters as quickly as possible. Whether it was this acceleration that caused the setbacks is unclear, but the troubles commenced from day one on set. The first mishap was when Karloff waded into the water below the destroyed windmill wearing a diver's suit under his costume. The whole outfit filled with water, expanded, and left Karloff floating around the lake unable to get to his feet. New costumes and a new diving suit were called for to allow the production to continue. The same day, the action moved to another sequence while they waited for the new threads. Karloff stepped out on a set piece, slipped and broke his hip. A few days earlier Clive broke his leg in a riding accident and other technical issues ensued during the production on various days thereafter. The whole photography schedule ended up being 10 days over program and $100,000 over budget. The same level of issues occurred during post-production. Whale was unhappy with sections and had them reshot, he also edited out over 15 minutes of footage that he didn't feel adequate for the story and then just days before the official premiere he completely reedited the final sequence.

One sequence that is a particular favorite of critics and fans alike is the scene where the Monster speaks to the blind man, as the pathos and emotion of the scene really sets the movie apart from the others being made at this time:

> Blind man: And now, for our lesson. Remember, this is bread.

> The Monster: Bread. (takes huge bite from the bread.)

> Blind man: And this is wine. (pours wine into mug). To drink.

The Monster: Drink. (Drinks wine and smiles) Good!
Good.

Blind Man: We are friends, you and I. Friends.

(Blind man & monster shake hands.)

The Monster: Friends.

(They both laugh happily)

The Monster: Good!

Blind man: And now for a smoke. (lights cigar.)

(Monster growls in fear.)

(Blind man laughs.)

Blind man: No, no. This is good. Smoke. You try.
(hands cigar to monster.)

The Monster: Smoke. (smokes cigar.) Good, good!
Good. (Hiccups, looks faint for a moment.)

Blind man: Before you came, I was all alone. It is bad to
be alone.

The Monster: Alone, bad. Friend, good. Friend, good!
(Shakes man's hand again, and they both laugh happily.)

Blind man: Now, come here. Tthey rise from the table
and walk across cabin. Blind man lifts a piece of wood.)
And what is this? (The Monster growls and shakes his
head.) This is wood, for the fire.

The Monster: Wood.

(Blind man leads monster towards fireplace.)

94

Blind man: And this is fire.

(The Monster growls and retreats.)

Blind man: No, no. Fire is good!

The Monster: Fire— no good!

Blind man: There is good, and there is bad.

The Monster: Good— bad?

The production made use of many of the original outdoor sets including the Court of Miracles and Little Europe. The laboratory was recreated on Stage 12 and the special effects used for filming the miniatures and the final destruction were all created on Stage 28.

The whole production had, in the eyes of the bosses at Universal, been a calamity from start to finish. This was reflected at the box-office when the movie was not as profitable as Universal had initially hoped, though it did finally bring a healthy profit margin of $950,000 sometime later. The movie was praised amongst critics, citing the director's brave technical and aesthetic alterations that made the movie appear fresh and new, despite it being a sequel. Others remarked on the movie's ability to showcase the talents of the cast and crew and how despite them working very independently and stylistically from one another they appeared to pull together to present a picture that was not your typical "monster of the month" movie. Variety praised the movie:

"Karloff manages to invest the character with some subtleties of emotion that are surprisingly real and touching. Thesiger as Dr Pretorious is a diabolic characterization if ever there was one and Lanchester

95

handles two assignments, being first in a preamble as author Mary Shelley and then the created woman. In latter assignment she impresses quite highly."

Despite the turmoil of the pre-production, the setbacks on set, and then the lackluster box-office receipts, the movie has grown in notoriety and is for many, an example of a sequel surpassing its predecessor to become a greater movie. It is identified by many modern day critics as being Whale's true masterpiece of his career, and one of the greatest examples of gothic filmmaking to ever be made in Hollywood. Topping the "best of" lists for many and even appearing in a huge number of "greatest ever movie" lists from the likes of Empire and others, it proves that this movie is standalone one of the greatest entries during Universal's golden era of monster movies.

The Bride being the anchor of the movie only appears onscreen for a short while and never appears again in another Universal Monster movie from this period. She has no dialogue and merely hisses throughout (an effect Lanchester said she was inspired to do from watching swans in Regents Park), though despite this apparent lack of screen time she has become one of a small number of iconic Universal Monsters. It is testament to the quality of Whale's production, the professionalism of the crew around him and the quality of the performances given that this movie really is set apart from many others.

Son of Frankenstein (1939)

The next major outing for the compounded colossus came just four years later with Son of Frankenstein. It would be one of the first Frankenstein movies made after the loss of the Laemmle's as the head of the corporation. The horror genre had been kicked to the long grass for a few years with the new management demanding more wholesome entertainment from the company. A combination of public demand and the re-running of the earlier movies (by theaters without the permission of Universal) forced their hand and by 1938 horror was once again back on the roster. This time, instead of cheap thrills it would be presented more lavishly and for this a higher budget was required.

Whale was first approached to bring the Monster back, but sharply declined, saying that his personal preference was to get back to making "any films bar horror." Instead, Universal appointed Robert V. Lee to take the helm. Lee was a widely experienced director who wasn't taken much within this genre. He had worked extensively on thrillers and gritty dramas, however, which would mean that he could easily bring some much-needed dynamism to the film. He ensured that rather than churning out another monster romp, he would in fact bring a more dramatic quality to the picture.

The story would focus on the son of Henry Frankenstein. A research doctor in his own right he soon finds his father's Monster in a coma and revives him. We subsequently find out later on in the movie that the Monster is in fact controlled by Ygor who is bent on revenge.

There were a number of alterations within this movie, despite apparently utilizing the same characters from the previous two movies. The Monster is now mute and is more monotonous as a character. Karloff had complained heavily that the Monster had spoken in the last picture, as he believed the Monster should always be mute. The director, taking notes from his star, must have agreed to this change. The look of the creature was fairly similar with the only major change being that he now wore a fur vest.

"Baron Wolf von Frankenstein: My son, herein lies my faiths, my beliefs and my enfoldments. A complete diary of my experiments, charts and secret formulas. In short, the sum total of my knowledge, such as it is. Perhaps you will regard my work with ridicule or even with a distaste. If so, destroy these records. But if you like me burn with the irresistible desire to penetrate the unknown, carry on. The path is cruel and torturous, carry on. I put secret after truth, you will be hated, blasphemed and condemned. You have inherited the fortune of the Frankensteins, I trust you will not inherit their fate."

Basil Rathbone was cast as Baron Wolf von Frankenstein; he was given the role after Peter Lorre had pulled out due to ill health. Rathbone, had just received massive plaudits for his role as Sir Guy of Gisbourne in The Adventures of Robin Hood and as Sherlock Holmes opposite Nigel Bruce. Bela Lugosi was also cast as the scheming Ygor, and for many his performance equaled that of any performances when he donned the famous vampire cloak.

It was decided upon very early into production that the movie should be shot in full Technicolor. An increased budget and the potential to make a livelier movie attracted the decision to make the movie in the first place. However, it was not to be and the plans to use the new technology fell through. Nobody knows the reasons behind the decision though speculation from the time said that the reason was a mix of budget costs and artistic differences. Some critics also point to the fact that the Monster may have appeared too horrific to audiences who were at the time just adjusting to the use of color at the cinema.

"That's true, but he'll find no friends here. Nothing but locked doors and darkened windows. Locked hearts and

bitter hatred. Let that, too, be a part of the Frankenstein heritage."

The production was for many a happy outing. Old work colleagues were back together, doing what they loved and the production overall was run with a pleasant and proactive mindset (Karloff's wife even had his first child while in the midst of this production). The production did not run as smoothly as Universal executives may have wanted, with the film running drastically over the agreed program. The reason for this is quite fascinating and had all to do with the falling star Bela Lugosi, who by this time was seeing his character trough (though he had many peaks and troughs throughout his career). He was out of work and needed a job. Lee, who was an old friend of the actor, quickly promised him a role within the picture and had his character written in and in fact by doing so, completely altered the entire script. Aware that Lugosi needed to work, they paid the poor actor a pittance based on a weekly rate for the weeks that he was needed on set to portray his character. What Universal did not know was that Lee worked it so that Ygor become central to the plot and thus he was needed on set for more weeks than first planned. In fact, Lee rewrote and redrafted so many scenes to give Lugosi more and more screen time that his paycheck was double what he had expected at the outset. Lugosi would be ever grateful to Lee for this assistance, as money aside, the redrafts allowed for Lugosi to adlib many of his scenes and thus allowed him to make the character far more than just a hunchbacked madman.

The effect of the increased budget could be clearly seen throughout the movie by way of extravagant sets and props that make the movie stand out from its franchise. The sets were designed by Jack Otterson who was a longstanding art director of particular note (he was nominated for an Academy Award eight times during his career). He built expressionist buildings with harsh lines and dark corners that enveloped the action and created shadows that could be the envy of any film noir from the time. The atmospheric architecture, combined with Lee's clever camerawork, the polished performances and a haunting new score by Frank Skinner combined to make a welcome addition to the Universal catalogue of monster movies. A side note about the opening sequence of this movie is that Orson Welles was so impressed with the visuals of this movie that it inspired him to recreate the same in Citizen Kane, which many critics believe to be the greatest movie of all time.

The Original 1939 US Theatrical Poster

Son of Frankenstein was a huge hit with audiences and would drag the company back into profitability at a time when the corporation was in desperate need of some success. Critics loved the new imagery; they noted the great performances and praised the high quality production from start to finish. The movie would also mark the last time that Karloff would play Frankenstein's Monster (though he did appear a few months later at a charity baseball match at the request of his friend and makeup authority Jack Pierce, and in an episode of the TV series Route 66 many years later in the 1960s). Karloff feared that the Monster was starting to become the brunt of jokes and that he would be typecast into the role without exploring other parts. The movie would also be the last time that such a large budget was spent on Frankenstein movies, and future versions would all squarely be considered B-movies.

The Ghost of Frankenstein (1942)

The fourth outing of the Monster would see the neck electrodes being passed to Universal mainstay Lon Chaney Jr. in 1941, with the movie being released in the following year. The story this time would see the scheming Ygor resurrecting the monster and bringing him to another son of Frankenstein with the purpose of resurrecting the Monster. Chaos ensues when again the brain is mixed up and the Monster breaks free.

The movie would also mark the final time the Monster headed his own individual movie; after this time the Monster would be installed within various "meets" or "rally" movies. The movie would see Ygor come back from the dead to exact his revenge, as supposedly the bullets that shot him dead in the previous feature only maimed him. Continuity errors such as this, plus the supposed never-mentioned second brother, actors performing more than one role, and other characters returning from the dead, all amounted to a far more cheapened final product than the previous features. The movie wholly lived up to its B-movie status.

In order to maintain this new factory approach to producing horror movies, it was decided that the movie required a director who was keen to work to budget expectations and who had a firm hand on program adherence, and that role fell to Erle C. Kenton. Kenton was a careful operator who in his working life had churned out some 130 movies between 1916 and 1957. He was a hard taskmaster and a safe pair of hands for the production; the type of person that Universal was keen to utilize to ensure the project was completed with no delays (unlike many of its higher budgeted predecessors). The movie would eventually be shot on time and on budget, though the noticeable lack of artistry is felt throughout.

"There's a curse upon this village... the curse of Frankenstein.

Aye. Aye, it is true.

The whole countryside shuns the village.

Our fields are barren, the inn is empty.

My little ones cry in their sleep.

They are hungry. There is no bread.

It's the curse, the curse of Frankenstein.

This is nonsense, folks.

You talk as though these were the Dark Ages.

You know as well as I do...that the monster died in the

sulphur pit under Frankenstein's tower...and that Ygor, his familiar...was riddled with bullets from the gun of Baron Frankenstein himself.

But Ygor does not die that easily.

They hanged him and broke his neck, but he lives.

Haven't I seen him, sitting beside the hardened sulphur pit playing his weird horn, as if to lure the monster back from death to do his evil bidding."

Lugosi returned to play Ygor. Initially Karloff was approached to return to play his most famous creature, but he declined and instead took up a part in Arsenic and Old Lace on Broadway. The Universal executives on hearing the news decided to appoint Lon Chaney Jr. into the role and to change the makeup and appearance of the classic character. Various tests were undertaken before it was decided that audiences might not take to a drastic change in the character's appearance, particularly as this was technically a sequel. Instead, the makeup was to remain the exact same and new pieces were made to fit Chaney's head. Chaney however, who was a known drinker at the time, did not like the fit and didn't have the patience of Karloff to sit for hours in the chair as they worked on him. One such day during filming, the headpiece was particularly irritating the actor. He complained to the director, who simply stated that production was close to an end for the day and that he should continue to wear the makeup until they knew they had shot enough for that day. Karloff demanded it be removed and the calls were ignored, so in frustration he grabbed the headpiece and tore it from his head throwing it at the ground. It was only later when removing the rest of the makeup that he realized that he had caused the skin to rip across his forehead leaving a nasty gash. Production was then shut down for three days whilst contingency plans were drawn up to reduce the amount of time they needed the Monster on set. The movie had already been delayed for several days a few weeks before, not long from the start of principal photography, when it was discovered that Chaney was allergic to the grease paint they used on his makeup.

"[the monster is struck by lightning]

Ygor: The lightning. It is good for you! Your father was Frankenstein, but your mother was the lightning!"

The movie overall is relatively exciting when compared to contemporary movies that were being produced at the same time on similar budgets. It never, however, quite met the audiences' expectations for a Frankenstein movie. This may have been because of the central actor's portrayal of the Monster, as Chaney played the character with little emotion or pathos and hobbled around the set groaning and lurching between scenes. The character is simply reduced to a mere murdering thug that is at the bidding of others. This did not resonate with audiences and provoked much discussion with the critics of the time. Two truncated 8mm versions of the movie were released in later decades; they were respectively named Frankenstein's New Brain and The Trial of Frankenstein.

Other appearances

The fifth Frankenstein movie would see the character become intertwined with the Wolf Man franchise. It was released in 1943 and again starred Bela Lugosi but this time, finally, as the Monster.

The movie would act as sequel to the original Wolf Man movie and, as the star, Lon Chaney Jr. had to swop from the platform boots to the hairy costume. This would necessitate Lugosi's portrayal of the character, some twelve years after he was originally attached to play the Monster. This was the final Universal monster movie in which the Monster played a major role; in the latter movies such as House of Frankenstein and House of Dracula, the Monster, played by Glenn Strange, comes to life only in the final scenes of each picture.

The next feature would be the House of Frankenstein released in 1945 and would see Karloff return to the franchise - not as his most famous creation, but instead as the title character Dr. Gustav Niemann. This mash up of various franchises would also see a sequel in House of Dracula in 1945, which would also feature the Monster, this time played by Glenn Strange. The movies at this point became very tongue in cheek and low budget. Karloff's warning about the character's descent into being the butt of the jokes was quickly seen in the deliberately farcical Abbott and Costello Meet Frankenstein (1948) where this time the Monster is but a henchman for other, more devious characters. The final time the Monster had appeared in these classic Universal pictures was in this comedy movie. It is then that he is finally given some dialogue, albeit just "Yes, master." It was also the last Universal monster flick to feature an actual member of the Frankenstein family as a character.

Abbott and Costello Meet Frankenstein (1948)

It was 1948 when Abbott and Costello Meet Frankenstein hit the big screen. William Abbot and Lou Costello were at the height of their popularity at the time. Having entertained the US with their vaudeville, stage, radio, television and film work, they were not only credited with being great entertainers, but with creating the medium of a duo comedy team working together for laughs. Abbot became the straight man, while Costello developed into the dimwitted, laugh-inducing partner. Though they started working together by chance when Costello's then-partner fell ill, they quickly realized how well they worked together and formed a duo. They starred in many films together and Abbott and Costello Meet Frankenstein was the twenty-first movie where they shared the stage. By 1948, when the movie was released, they were well known and could easily carry a large budget film on their own.

The movie started filming on February 5, 1948. Bud Abbot was cast as Chick Young and Lou Costello was Wilbur Grey. Both characters were baggage handlers tasked with delivering boxes of Count Dracula and Frankenstein monsters to the wax museum. Of course things didn't go as planned, which is where the favorite duo played out their usual shtick to adoring audiences.

> "Wilbur Grey: Well that's gonna cost you overtime because I'm a union man and I work only sixteen hours a day.
>
> McDougal: A union man only works eight hours a day.
>
> Wilbur Grey: I belong to two unions."

Production scheduling was to last for about nine weeks. Rumor has it that the stars weren't big fans of their movie vehicle. In fact, Lou Costello was heard saying that his five-year-old could have created a better script. He slowly changed his mind though and went through with the project. His early disdain for the movie quickly dissipated once filming began and he was able to have fun on set. Actor Glen Strange, who portrayed the actual monster of Frankenstein, said that it was difficult for him to keep a straight face with Costello purposely making him laugh. The lightheartedness of the set also was noted throughout the many pie-in-the-face fights the cast and crew had in between filming.

The studio also added to the tongue-in-cheek feel by writing popular actors into the film with bit parts. Bela Lugosi returned to his signature character Dracula; he had originally portrayed the role in 1931 when it made him a bona fide star. Lon Chaney Jr. took on his signature character of the Wolf Man and famous actor Vincent Price made a vocal appearance as the Invisible Man. Boris Karloff also let the studio take pictures of him in line waiting to purchase a ticket to the film as another promotional gag (though he didn't star in the picture).

In terms of writing the script, it took a few rewrites to get approval from Universal to go ahead with filming. Initially the script was written by Oscar Brodney. Though he had the basics down, the studio wanted some changes and brought in Bertram Milhauser who has already written successful Sherlock Holmes films for Universal. He was known to be a detail-oriented writer who could weave small details that contributed to the authenticity and intrigue within a movie. Despite his expertise, his work was also not approved by the studio.

> "Dracula: And about the brain? I don't want to repeat
> Frankenstein's mistake and revive a vicious,
> unmanageable brute. This time the Monster must have no
> will of his own, no fiendish intellect to oppose his Master."

Writers Robert Lees and Frederick I. Rinaldo were next brought in to write a screenplay. They came up with the final script and it was approved by Universal Studios. The actors, sans Costello, also liked the direction it took. Originally entitled The Brain of

Frankenstein, it was a complex story and was watered down. Despite difficulties, they eventually managed to deliver an acceptable script.

As stated, Costello wasn't sold on the script and immediately showed his disapproval to producer Robert Arthur by storming into his office. Arthur recalled in an interview having to coerce Costello into the movie, promising him that he could have his chosen director work with him on the film and reminding him of the financial gain it likely would provide. Projections were positive and that's why the studio was willing to take a chance on the comedy duo. They were at the height of their success and it was a formula that had worked time and time again in previous movies.

On set, actors Abbott and Costello were the usual jokesters. They orchestrated numerous daily practical jokes on the cast and crew. They also held card games and engaged in fun activities to quell the boredom of filming a movie. Not all of the actors were entertained though. Bela Lugosi came from a completely different school of acting where pranks, fun and games, and revelry were not acceptable. The role that made his career was his 1931 portrayal of Dracula and he believed that frightening people was his sole and highly-respectable purpose in movies. To act otherwise would be a "blemish" on his reputation. Of course Abbott and Costello were the true comedy team that wanted to make everyone laugh and have a good time. Regardless of their audience - whether it was an auditorium of 1,000 people or a crew of 20 - their goal was the same. Lugosi was not amused, often sitting on the sidelines glaring at them with total disgust when the duo began their joking.

At one point during the filming of the movie, Lenore Aubert, who portrayed Dr. Sandra Mornay, took Strange in his Frankenstein's monster makeup along with Lon in his Wolf Man makeup for a walk around Universal Studios. Tours were always being offered during the days so a group of tourists who were visiting saw an unusual sight when they saw Aubert guiding the Wolf Man and

Frankenstein's monster around the studio's lot with the help of leashes. Again, fun and games were the order of the day according to the cast. They definitely didn't disappoint!

The movie was considered to be a big-budget film for the time. The total cost for the movie was $800,000. In today's world that would be scoffed at, but for the year 1948 that was a huge investment. A large portion of the budget was attributed to the sets that were created to be eerily spooky. Dracula's castle was particularly expensive to replicate. Also, in the movie there is a scene where Dracula morphs into a bat. This took the latest technology and animation to carry off. Combined with special makeup, it made the effect as realistic and intriguing as possible for the day.

There were some changes in the character's makeup that also altered the budget. Because so much money was put into the sets and special effects, other elements were dialed down in cost. One place where costs were cut considerably was with actors' makeup. In previous films the Wolf Man and Frankenstein both had intricate and uncomfortable makeup. For this production, the studio decided to go with much more convenient options. Quick-change rubber sponge masks were used to create the movie monsters. This allowed actors to get ready within an hour for on-camera work.

"Wilbur Grey: Mr. Talbot, and I thought you were such a nice man too. Look at you, you're a mess.

Larry Talbot: Last night I went through another one of my horrible experiences. Many years ago I was bitten by a werewolf. Now, whenever the full moon rises I turn into a wolf myself.

Wilbur Grey: Oh pal. That's all right; I'm sort of a wolf

myself."

Throughout production, there were some issues. Actor Glenn Strange, who portrayed the Frankenstein Monster, had a difficult time keeping a straight face with Costello around. He claimed that the actor was so funny that maintaining a fearsome stance of a monster was next to impossible. It was clear to see that this was an issue when, during the film, Costello sits abruptly on the monster's lap. The monster is seen chuckling under makeup. Also, Strange had a larger issue with filming when he inadvertently stepped on a camera cable and caused it to fall on his foot, breaking bones. Lon Chaney Jr. had to step in and portray the Frankenstein monster. Boris Karloff was also adamant about not appearing with Abbott and Costello in the movie, though he agreed to do publicity for the movie. Interestingly enough, he already had appeared with them in the film Abbott and Costello Meet the Killer Boris Karloff and also in Abbott and Costello Meet Dr. Jekyll and Mr. Hyde. Why the third film was not to his liking was never revealed.

The Cast of Abbott and Costello Meet Frankenstein

Overall, the production went smoothly, apart from a few bumps. They were quickly dealt with, though, to keep filming on track and get the completed version to the viewing public.

When Abbott and Costello Meet Frankenstein came out, some critics stated that the studio had hit rock bottom by having respected monsters play against Abbot and Costello's light slapstick routine. Though some critics weren't fans of the movie, claiming that it denigrated the horror film industry, Abbot and Costello were used to carrying horror. One of their firmly established film routines was to play the unknowing duo who faced off inadvertently against the monster. They played it out in earlier films like Hold that Ghost and Zombies on Broadway. Both solidified the standard mix of the comedy duo with scary monsters.

These negative reviews definitely were the minority though. Big-name publications such as Variety and The New York Star reported that it was a fantastic success. What made the film so successful, according to these critics, was the antics of Abbott and Costello. Though Lugosi wouldn't agree, the reviewers called it zany, fun and with a touch of fright - exactly what the market called for at the time. They also stated that no one could oust the comedy duo from any production because of how well they worked together. In the medium of horror, they were perfect at playing their standard characters of a bumbling idiot and the straight-man trying to stay out of trouble.

Though there was some buzz that comedy mixed with horror tarnished the latter, it was definitely unfounded and a matter of sole opinion. In the end, the film that closed with a production budget of approximately $792,000 ended up earning $2.2m. Its stars Abbott and Costello were paid $105,000 each.

Abbott and Costello Meet Frankenstein became a classic. This was partially because of the many cameos and the success of the film, but primarily because of the two main stars who had defined the comedic duo market. For years to come their work and synergy would influence comics and actors. This is just one example of how well the two worked together and how much they contributed to the world of film throughout the 1940s and 1950s in America. Today the film is loved by both horror and comedy fans.

> "Chick Young: Now listen, Talbot. Enough is enough. Now Wilbur's scared to death. Hello? Hello? He's gone.
>
> Wilbur: So am I.
>
> Chick Young: No you don't come here. I'm gonna settle this thing once and for all. We'll search this place.
>
> Wilbur: Look Chick, it's a little past sunset and if Dracula is here he's gonna be wanting breakfast, and I'm fatter than you, and it ain't gonna be me."

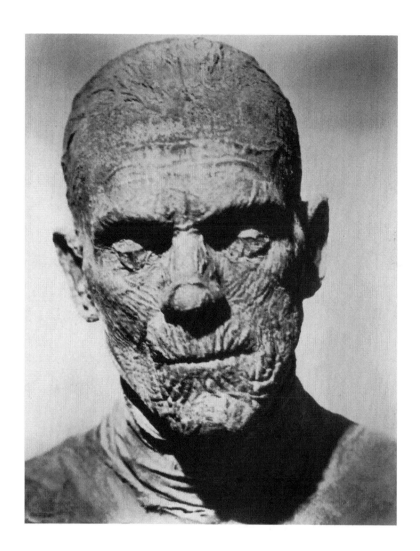

THE MUMMY

"Curious Occurrence in the Louvre. — Yesterday morning a strange discovery was made in the principal Egyptian Chamber. The ouvriers who are employed to clean out the rooms in the morning found one of the attendants lying dead upon the floor with his arms round one of the mummies. So close was his embrace that it was only with the utmost difficulty that they were separated. One of the cases containing valuable rings had been opened and rifled. The authorities are of opinion that the man was bearing away the mummy with some idea of selling it to a private collector, but that he was struck down in the very act by longstanding disease of the heart. It is said that he was a man of uncertain age and eccentric habits, without any living relations to mourn over his dramatic and untimely end."

The Ring of Thoth by Sir Arthur Conan Doyle.

Egyptian origins

Late afternoon on November 4th 1922 the British archaeologist Howard Carter uncovered the find of a lifetime. It had taken him over eighteen years to locate but he had finally discovered the tomb of Tutankhamun. The ruler of Egypt in the 18th Dynasty was a little-known pharaoh who left little imprint on history during his lifetime; it would however be the discovery of his tomb that would cause the greatest fascination. His tomb, which had been untouched for over three thousand years, would be opened for the first time by Carter and his associate Lord Carnarvon, with this moment in history eventually creating "Tut-mania."

Carter became fascinated with finding the tomb of this lesser-known leader as it had never been located. In fact, many believed the tomb didn't exist in the first place owing to his minimal impact on history; however, this did not deter Carter at all. At the time, his find was made all that more special due to the fact that scores of other such tombs had long been raided by jewel thieves and antiquarians searching for riches. The discovery of this wholly untouched and fully complete tomb was made all the more fascinating owing to this fact. Searching through ancient manuscripts and using his expert knowledge of hieroglyphics Carter managed to piece together the exact location of the tomb, a task that took years to do and was also delayed due to the First World War. In fact, many thought in the summer of 1922 that the quest was to be fruitless, and his associate Carnarvon, who was funding the expedition, nearly pulled the funding during these months.

The Pyramids of the ancient Pharaohs

A crew of local laborers was sourced and they were deployed to dig around an area specified by Carter. They labored long into the hot days, finding very little. Carter, frustrated at the lack of progress, started to review his notes to see if there were any additional clues to the location of the tomb. It was after many exhaustive days that he realized he had discounted a section of land purely because it had been searched by another archaeological team. He quickly decided to re-look at this area due to the fact that the former team had not quite searched this area adequately enough. The other crew had less labor and was perhaps slightly haphazard in their investigation. This switching of sites and moving of labor angered Carnarvon who started to doubt that Carter actually knew that this tomb existed here. Digging down past some huts that had been temporarily erected they found lots of large boulders – something that was very curious owing to the fact that these stones had been previously heavily worked on and tooled. Upon clearing the boulders, they found some stone steps cut into the bedrock. These sixteen or so steps led down into an arched doorway with a mud-covered walling within a plastered aperture, stamped with indistinct oval seals called cartouches. Carnarvon, who had by this time left for England, was quickly telegrammed and within a few days returned with his daughter Lady Evelyn Herbert. The trio could not be more ecstatic over the find.

Carter had temporarily placed some of the boulders back to seal the doorway to wait for his associate and backer (plus daughter) to return. The day they arrived, he instructed the laborers to remove the rocks from the stairway, clear the seals and allow them in to investigate. Around the door Carter quickly found the name "Tutankhamun" carved into the stone. Closer inspection revealed that Carter and his team had not been the first to enter into the tomb as the doorway showed signs that it had been breached and resealed at least twice. Initially the team was disappointed, but further examination revealed that the breaches must have occurred shortly after the burial by Egyptian citizens wishing to steal the dead pharaoh's gold and jewels. They were likely caught, executed, and the doorway resealed. Eventually over time people lost interest in raiding the tomb, owing to the ultimate punishment that would be inflicted upon them. As the centuries went by, the tomb had finally been lost to time until Carter's team arrived in the 1920s.

They prised the doorway open and found a long tunnel with hieroglyphics that warned grave robbers of their fate should they disturb this tomb. Ignoring the warnings, they continued down to another doorway that had been resealed in the same manner as the previous. Not wanting to disturb this evidence and owing to their position below ground, Carter made a hole in the door and used his candle to check for poisonous gases before entering inside.

> "Slowly, desperately slowly it seemed to us as we watched, the remains of passage debris that encumbered the lower part of the doorway were removed, until at last we had the whole door clear before us. The decisive moment had arrived. With trembling hands I made a tiny breach in the upper left hand corner. Darkness and blank space, as far as an iron testing-rod could reach, showed that whatever lay beyond was empty, and not filled like the passage we had just cleared. Candle tests were applied as a precaution against possible foul gases, and then, widening the hole a little, I inserted the candle and peered in, Lord Carnarvon, Lady Evelyn [Lord Carnarvon's daughter] and Callender [an assistant] standing anxiously beside me to hear the verdict. At first I could see nothing, the hot air escaping from the chamber causing the candle flame to flicker, but presently, as my eyes grew accustomed to the light, details of the room within emerged slowly from the mist, strange animals, statues, and gold - everywhere the glint of gold. For the moment - an eternity it must have seemed to the others standing by - I was struck dumb with amazement, and when Lord Carnarvon, unable to stand the suspense any longer,

inquired anxiously, 'Can you see anything?' it was all I could do to get out the words, 'Yes, wonderful things.' Then widening the hole a little further, so that we both could see, we inserted an electric torch..."

Howard Carter recounting the entry in 1923

The "wonderful things" that glinted in the candlelight from the small doorway would eventually be seen as one of the greatest ever ancient Egyptian discoveries. Beyond what he could see at this point lay other rooms with various artifacts and jewels. All manner of treasures adorned the rooms; so much in fact, that it took the team over two months to carefully catalogue and sort all the items they found. It was after a few weeks that a final room was found at the back of the chamber. This would have to be the final resting place of the body of King Tutankhamun, which according to legend was buried within a golden casket. Carter and his assistant carefully began to chip away at the sealed door, a door that had never been opened at all, not even by the ancient tomb raiders. Carter recounts:

"My first care was to locate the wooden lintel above the door: then very carefully I chipped away the plaster and picked out the small stones which formed the uppermost layer of the filling. The temptation to stop and peer inside at every moment was irresistible, and when, after about ten minutes' work, I had made a hole large enough to enable me to do so, I inserted an electric torch. An astonishing sight its light revealed, for there, within a yard of the doorway, stretching as far as one could see and blocking the entrance to the chamber, stood what to all appearances was a solid wall of gold. For the moment there was no clue as to it's meaning, so as quickly as I

dared I set to work to widen the hole..."

Howard Carter recounting the entry in 1923

Carter carefully removed the few remaining stones to make a hole big enough for him to enter. As he slowly entered, holding just an electric torch, he soon discovered that the "wall of gold" was in fact an outsized gold shrine built to honor the Pharaoh, but to also protect his sarcophagus. Some stones had collapsed in the chamber and when these were carefully removed a beautiful gilded surface was revealed. Carter and his crew's excitement spread from the camp and soon the outside world would want to see what they had discovered.

"It was, beyond any question, the sepulchral chamber in which we stood, for there, towering above us, was one of the great gilt shrines beneath which kings were laid. So enormous was this structure (17 feet by 11 feet, and 9 feet high, we found afterwards) that it filled within a little the entire area of the chamber, a space of some two feet only separating it from the walls on all four sides, while its roof, with cornice top and torus moulding, reached almost to the ceiling. From top to bottom it was overlaid with gold, and upon its sides there were inlaid panels of brilliant blue faience, in which were represented, repeated over and over, the magic symbols which would ensure its strength and safety. Around the shrine, resting upon the ground, there were a number of funerary emblems, and, at the north end, the seven magic oars the king would need to ferry himself across the waters of the underworld. The walls of the chamber, unlike those of the Antechamber, were decorated with brightly painted scenes and inscriptions, brilliant in their colours, but evidently

somewhat hastily executed."

Howard Carter recounting the entry in 1923

Newspapers around the world soon ran the story of the plucky archaeologist, and this garnered media attention from every corner. This created the "Tut-mania" of the 1920s, as previously mentioned, and ensured Carter would become a kind of celebrity of his day. The other idea that was perpetuated at the time was the idea of "The Mummy's Curse" or "Tutankhamun's Curse." Journalists covering the dig at the time exploited the fact that a number of warnings were found in the tunnel at the entrance to the tomb, with these warnings of death and injury to the disturbers of this tomb creating a number of column inches. It was these inches that were soon to become whole pages when member of the crew started to experience a great number of inauspicious events.

An example of the hieroglyphics that were found

The renowned Egyptologist James Henry Breasted worked with Carter soon after the discovery. An expert in hieroglyphics, he was brought in to help Carter account for all the items painted onto the walls and ceilings within the tomb. He would recount the first utterance of the potential curse on site at the dig. He recalled that the day after he arrived (which was soon after the first doorway was breached), Carter had retired to his tent when a shriek rang out at the campsite. Carter's pet canary had been eaten by a cobra that had slithered inside his cage and swallowed the bird whole. Laborers on the site spoke among their ranks to warn themselves and others that the cobra confined within a gilded cage was the ancient symbol of the Egyptian monarchy. These hushed discussions soon spread to the local villages where it was feared that Carter and his team had awoken "an ancient curse" by finding the tomb. Arthur Weigall, a former antiquarian inspector working for the Egyptian government recounted in his journal of the time that the cobra striking the bird within the cage was symbolic of the "Royal Cobra," which was used to decorate the headpieces of Egyptian Pharaohs. The cobra would symbolize the quiet strength of the ancient rulers in the face of adversity. The timing, Weigall wrote, was the symbolic entry Carter had done to the ancient tomb that very day.

The next cursed incident came from the mysterious death of Carter's main associate and backer, Lord Carnarvon. A mosquito had bitten him soon after he had returned to the site, when the tomb was first opened. The bite had been to his face, and when shaving a few days later, he happened to nick the bite with his razor. The bite became infected and he entered into a brief period of unconsciousness before dying one afternoon. A doctor was called and he ruled that Lord Carnarvon had died from blood poisoning caused by the wound. Two weeks after his death, a letter was written by Marie Corelli who had been visiting the site. The letter was published in the New York World magazine and spoke of the "dire punishment" that would befall anyone who had entered into the ancient tomb. This sparked a mass media frenzy that soon reported that the supposed curse was a punishment for the team for unearthing the tomb. Soon after, museums and private collectors who had amassed collections from other tombs started to question the validity of this letter's sources. Some however, were far more cautionary, with one prominent member of the Egyptian government taking a mummy he had received as a gift off from display at a nearby official building.

An ancient Egyptian burial chamber

Sir Arthur Conan Doyle, creator of the Sherlock Holmes stories, suggested that Lord Carnarvon's death was the result of spirits that had been created by Tutankhamun's priests to guard his tomb; this commentary by the celebrated author further fueled the media frenzy that was rampant at this time. Weigall, who had kept a thorough diary of his visits to the site, wrote within his journal at the time of the opening that the Lord's manner upon which he entered ensured that he would "receive only six weeks to live."

The mystery deepened when it was discovered that Tutankhamun too might have died from a mosquito bite. An autopsy carried out on the well-preserved remains of the deceased Pharaoh indicated that he had some form of lesion to his left cheek. It was hypothesized by many, but mainly the media, that King Tut had carried out his revenge on the Lord for backing this whole operation by killing him in the manner in which he had met his own death. Neither notes taken from the Lord's coroner or the surviving autopsy report can confirm whether the lesion or the mosquito bite were located on the exact same place on each face.

Tutankhamun's mask, now showcased in the Egyptian Museum in Cairo

Some weeks later the site was visited by George Jay Gould, who visited after hearing the news of the discovery. He left and a few days later was reported to have died from a fever that his family believed he had picked up whilst visiting Egypt. Later Prince Ali Kamel Fahmy Bey of Egypt died during the initial cataloguing of the site, having been shot dead by his wife. Though not in attendance, Colonel Aubrey Herbert, MP, Lord Carnarvon's half-brother, became nearly blind and died a few weeks later from blood poisoning related to a dental procedure intended to restore his eyesight. He had only just inherited his brother's title when he died from this unexpected cause. A further incident came a year later when anthropologist Henry Field visited the site to meet with Carter and to see the treasures for himself. He reported that Carter had gifted a friend of his, Sir Bruce Ingram, with a paperweight that was put together from a mummified hand that held a bracelet which read "Cursed be he who moves my body. To him shall come fire, water and pestilence." A month after receiving the gift it was then reported that Ingram's house was razed to the ground when a fire broke out in the servants' quarters. It was subsequently rebuilt, only to be flooded on completion.

Other events of the supposed curse include:

- Sir Archibald Douglas-Reid's mysterious illness in 1924. He died shortly after being the principle radiologist in charge of scanning Tutankhamun's mummy.
- Sir Lee Stack, who was Governor-General of Sudan, died in the same year on a visit to Cairo. He had been assassinated whist driving through the nearby capital city.
- Lord Carnarvon's other brother would die a few years later from pneumonia.
- A. C. Mace, an assistant working for Carter during the expedition, died four years after the initial entry into the tomb from arsenic poisoning.
- Captain Richard Bethell who was Carter's personal secretary died in 1929 from eating poison that had been applied to some food he ate in bed one night. His father

also died when only a few months later he mysteriously fell from his seventh floor apartment.

Other than the prominent entries above, there are over twenty deaths that are supposed "victims of the curse" not listed here. Carter did, however, mention within his diaries the following:

"We were totally unprepared for such a large quantity of visitors, and in view of the preservation of the antiquities they being very crowded and in poor preservation, we were obliged to refuse admission until some preparation was made to safeguard the objects."

So it is likely that the huge numbers of visitors coming to site just combined with a series of unfortunate events. Carter himself believed the curse to be entirely imaginary, although following the cobra found in his pet canary's cage, he did witness one extremely odd sighting. Some days after the cobra debacle, he was walking back to his tent when a pack of jackals ran past him into the desert. He noted that the heads of the animals resembled that of Anubis, who was the guardian of the dead in ancient Egypt. A report that he said was made all the stranger as he had never seen such an animal in all the thirty-plus years he had been living and working in the Egyptian deserts.

The mythology of the mummy and the connotations of reanimation via the supernatural had been an invention of the literary world in the nineteenth century. Ancient Egyptians, however, did not believe this to be a possibility. The mummification of the body for a celebrated leader was designed to be undertaken for the afterlife and not for any terrestrial reasons. The remains were prepared in this manner to serve as a link between the physical being and the spirit, and it just so happens that the method would preserve the remains relatively well for centuries. The ancient Egyptians as part of the process would remove vital organs to facilitate the transfer from one world to the next, so this removal of the brains or the eyes would render any potential mummified corpse somewhat ineffective should it be proposed to walk the Earth again. This plot hole would actually be answered in a number of movies, no less the Universal ones, where a plot device is borrowed from a Victorian novel to facilitate this omission. In Cleopatra (1889) by H. Rider Haggard, it is explained that the mummy is able to return as he had not been buried correctly and had in fact been buried alive, thus with his organs intact. This plot device would be seen in a great number of different mummy pictures.

One of the very first stories to be printed that featured supernatural reanimated mummies, as we know them today, was published in 1827, entitled The Mummy! by J. Webb. Set in the future, the book acts more as a moral code against the ills of Frankenstein where instead of dealing out brutish murders, the monster in question actually advises on politics and religion and is quite rational.

> "On the winding up of his affairs that it would be necessary to do something for my support. I had written a strange, wild novel, called the Mummy, in which I had laid the scene in the twenty-second century, and attempted to predict the state of improvement to which this country might possibly arrive."

> Jane Webb on her novel The Mummy!

Edgar Allan Poe would produce Some Words with a Mummy in 1845, where a mummy is revived with electricity, borrowing the central premise from Frankenstein. This work could be considered the first classic mummy tale that would be recognizable to audiences today. Like Webb's novel, the book features a public "unwrapping show" a popular event for the curious people of the Victorian era when mummies were publicly unwrapped and analyzed for the paying public. The work is only a short story and talks a lot about the perception of religion and God. Another great title from this time is Théophile Gautier's The Romance of the Mummy that was first published in 1858. This work acts in a similar manner to the others though it was the first to introduce the idea of love across the centuries. Gautier wrote a sequel in 1863 entitled The Mummy's Foot which is about an archaeologist who returns to England from Egypt and uses a mummy's foot as a paperweight and then dreams of the mummy returning from the afterlife to reclaim his lost appendage. It wasn't until 1897 with Richard Marsh's The Beetle that the first use of revenge from defilement of a mummy's grave is used as main plot device. Many of these ideas would be bound together and presented most successfully by Arthur Conan Doyle in his works The Ring of Thoth (1890) and Lot No. 249 (1892). It would be these two works that would heavily inspire Universal many years later.

Early Mummy movies

As you will see with Universal's impressive run of later Mummy movies, there has been a great interest in the empirical undead. This interest may have started with "Tut-mania," but it did however continue right through the early beginnings of the cinema right up to the Universal version. Before the Universal version was made, over forty different pictures had been produced around the world, starting as early as 1899 with Georges Méliès' Cleopatra where the female pharaoh is brought back to life. Even Walt Disney cashed in on the popular theme by producing a Silly

Symphony cartoon called Egyptian Melodies that features dancing mummies in a pyramid.

The Edison Company (whom we mentioned in the Frankenstein chapter) also provided the world with two different Mummy movies during their tenure. Naidra, The Dream Worker and the later The Necklace of Rameses were both similar movies where the main protagonist steals from the burial chamber of various mummified pharaohs and then panics when they believe the curse of the respective mummies is coming for them. Both films were made in the 1910s. The 1914 film version of Through the Centuries directed by F. Huntley featured a story that was reminiscent of Conan Doyle's work and features a 3000-year-old high princess who is reincarnated and brought back to life via her lover. A similar theme was present in director Maurice Tourneur's The Undying Flame in 1917; this is similar to Universal's version as the ancient pharaoh princess is reanimated into the body of modern day woman.

The Mummy (1932)

Following the tremendous success of both Dracula and then Frankenstein, Carl Laemmle Jr. was keen to get another monster flick straight into production. He soon commissioned Richard Schayer to find a literary source from which he could mine a great screenplay. "Tut-mania" was still attracting column inches in a number of newspapers worldwide, popularized mostly by Carter himself vowing to attract further backers to his research. Schayer believed that the curse that was being reported on would make a fine idea for a potential monster movie. He searched in nearby Los Angeles libraries for ideas. He soon happened upon a story contained within the anthology The Captain of the Polestar, and Other Tales by Sir Arthur Conan Doyle (who himself was equally fascinated with all the happenings in Egypt). It would be the short story from this book called "The Ring of Thoth" that first inspired the Hollywood producers, which was a story of strange happenings occurring within a museum. Using this as a foundation for their research they also found Alessandro Cagliostro had written a nine-page treatment entitled Cagliostro. The story was of an ancient magician who survives living in modern day California by injecting himself with nitrates to stay alive. Schayer thought that they could capitalize on the ongoing media interest in the Egyptian curse by creating a movie around these specific elements and presented Laemmle with the ideas. Laemmle soon agreed and he hired John L. Balderston to write the script. Balderston had been hired as he had worked on the previous two scripts for the other monster movies and proved to have quite a good track record for producing high quality scripts. What Laemmle didn't know was that Balderston had actually worked as a journalist based in London and had covered the initial reports of the tomb's opening at the British branch of the magazine New York World. Balderston turned out to be the perfect appointee for the project, as he would have firsthand knowledge of the expedition along with firsthand accounts from meeting with people who had been at the dig. This would ensure that he wrote a script that was not just dramatically excellent but was also packed with authentic elements that mirrored rea-life occurrences.

Balderston would move the initial story from modern day California to Egypt and rename the title character as Imhotep after the ancient Egyptian architect of the same name. He also changed the main motives of the central character from revenge to lost love. In the original treatment of the idea that Schayer had presented, he had wanted a story where the mummy would rise and take revenge on all the women who resembled his own former lover. This would instead be changed to a plot where the mummy has risen after being disturbed to revive his lost lover by mummifying her reincarnated self. Balderston created the Scroll of Thoth (in a nod to Conan Doyle), to create some authenticity to the script. In ancient mythology, Thoth was also said to have created the "Book of the dead," which added to the movie's authenticity.

Unlike previous movies that Universal had made, this one would be specifically written with Boris Karloff in mind to play the ancient pharaoh. Karloff was attached to the project even before Frankenstein had been officially released and only the working titles existed; this was due in part to the fact that Laemmle wanted to build on the marketing buzz surrounding his first two Monster pictures. The combination of his patience for makeup, his tormented expressions and fine character acting would ensure that Karloff would be a popular choice for the role and would keep him ably employed for years to come.

Karl Freund was hired to direct the picture. He had previously worked as the cinematographer on the earlier Dracula but he had been a prolific director in his native Germany during the early years of cinema. It was at this point that the movie was retitled from the working title of The King of the Dead to The Mummy. Filming would be scheduled for three solid weeks with a rigorous production schedule drafted. The very first scene shot at the Universal backlot was the reanimation scene where Karloff had endured hours in the makeup chair with his old friend Jack Pierce. Pierce had studied photos taken by early photographers cataloguing the tombs of the pharaohs; the final look of Karloff for the production would be that of Ramesses III as Pierce had decided that the facial features of both men had a degree of similarity between them. Karloff would be called to the makeup chair at 11am, where cotton would be applied along with spirit gum and clay into his hair. Bandages would then be applied which had been treated with acid to give them the aged look of the movie. The makeup would be complete by 7pm that same day allowing Karloff to film these scenes at night until 2am before taking two hours to carefully remove them; often he would not leave the lot until 5am. Though many successors of the Frankenstein makeup would complain of the tedious and sometimes painful nature of the application for their movies, it would Karloff's turn to complain about the pain endured when removing the makeup from his role in this picture. The removal of the gum in particular was said to be incredibly painful and would sometimes leave blotches on his face. He would later recall that the process, including the timings, would be "the most trying ordeal I had ever endured." The image of Karloff as the Mummy is as iconic as any other Universal picture ever made, but it is a fact that the image of Karloff as the Mummy appears only briefly in the film despite the great lengths and pains that he and the production team went to in order to present as authentic representation of the creature as possible. Pierce's efforts paid off (and Karloff's patience!) as Pierce was honored by a makeup award for his efforts at a ceremony that included his muse Karloff presenting it to him shortly after the release. The trophy that came with the award was thought to be lost following Pierce's death in 1968, however nearly ten years later it was discovered behind a sink in the makeup department when the sink was leaking and needed replacing.

Freund ensured that the script and the production schedule were followed exactly, with customary German precision. Freund can also be praised for two noticeable innovations that were made in order to make the picture seem more authentic. The first was in the composition of a thorough musical score. Unlike its Monster predecessors, Freund begged Laemmle to allow him the opportunity to utilize the sound in the picture to its greatest potential. Laemmle agreed and Freund appointed James Dietrich who, despite scoring the whole picture, worked closely with Freund to ensure that he crafted tracks to Freund's exacting demands for the picture. Some instances can be seen, however, where Freund trashed his colleague's work and replaced them with stock music from the Universal library. One notable example is the opening credits where Dietrich's score was replaced with Tchaikovsky's Swan Lake theme – a piece that had accompanied the opening of Dracula too. The other innovation for the picture was the use of a new technology called "back projection" which was an historic method of projecting actors into different settings from the ones they stood currently in, a kind of crude "blue/green screen" in today's terminology. Various scenes were shot in Cairo by second unit teams, which were then edited into the action being filmed on Universal's backlot. An example of this is where the filming from a car is undertaken in Cairo then projected onto a screen behind a similar vehicle back on the sound stage to depict a moving vehicle (a method still widely used today, particularly for sitcoms). Freund had experimented with this technique before, but this was the first time such technology had been used in the Hollywood cinema.

Karloff in full Mummy makeup

The budget for the picture was just under $200,000, which is less than the previous monster flicks that Universal had put out. The whole picture as it is presented today, save the second unit footage, was all shot on Universal's backlot. There was however one additional sequence that was filmed out in the Mojave Desert somewhere between the state lines of California and Nevada. The sequence was shot but was then edited out at the last minute from the final movie. The sequence is believed to show the brief events leading up to Karloff's mummification. It was believed that as the scenes showed a variety of ancient religious-type ceremonies it should be cut to avoid any sacrilegious overtones with the Censors. The sequence has actually been lost to time from the Universal archives. All that remains are a handful of production stills of the shoot with the sand and rocks of the local desert dressed to appear as the sand dunes of the Sahara Desert. There was also a brief mention in the titles of "Saxon Warrior" played by Henry Victor – a part that was completely cut as it was wholly contained within this sequence.

The movie was heavily marketed on the back of the success of the former Monster pictures that preceded it. Publicity around the Western world proclaimed that "Karloff the Uncanny" was back to frighten and delight audiences. In New York a huge billboard was erected in Times Square advertising the picture. Cinemas were paid to have actors dressed as mummies stalking the lobbies, and mummy merchandise and mummy theming adorned theaters across the country. The world had seen "Tut-mania," now it was experiencing Universal's "mummy mania." The movie became a box-office hit, with audiences flocking to see Karloff in another monster epic. The cinema returns seemed to be particularly high in the UK which at this time seemed to have been the epicenter of "Tut-mania."

The Mummy's Hand (1940)

Unlike both Dracula and Frankenstein, The Mummy did not have a direct sequel but rather a number of pictures that shared the same themes. The next chronological mummy movie from 1940 was a loose remake called The Mummy's Hand. The story followed the adventure of two unemployed archaeologists in Egypt who discover the burial site of an ancient Egyptian princess. After receiving funding from a wealthy magician they and the magician's daughter set out to investigate the site further. They are prevented by an ancient curse in the form of a sinister high priest and mummy (the latter played by Tom Tyler), both of whom are sworn to protect the tomb from outside raiders. Tyler was picked by Universal to play the part of the mummy, his only ever horror appearance, as he was the exact same height and build as Karloff. And although he also went through the grueling makeup processes of Pierce (and he had more screen time as the mummy than Karloff!), he was allowed to wear a crude rubber mask for any long shots or rapid sequences.

> "The High Priest: For who shall defile the temples of the ancient gods, a cruel and violent death shall be his fate, and never shall his soul find rest unto eternity. Such is the curse of Amon-Ra, king of all the gods."

Despite being a loose remake of the original, the picture was very firmly a B-movie picture that replaced high drama with audience thrills, and the lavish set decorations were also scaled back to produce a crowd pleasing but cost-effective picture. The whole movie was made for just $80,000 and was shot entirely on Universal's backlot. The excavation scenes for example were shot in a rocky section of the land near the natural hills at the rear of the studio that is now known as "Gausman's Gulch"; an area named after Russell A. Gausman who worked as set decorator for this and many other of the monster movies. The area was used extensively for any rocky terrain or desert-like settings that were required for a variety of movies. Its wild appearance was added to by the placing of papier-mâché boulders and artificial rocks that were easily replicated and used instead of the expense of moving productions out into the Californian deserts. Reusing footage already shot for its predecessor complemented the onsite ingenuity. Eagle-eyed fans of the picture did notice Karloff in the background of some of these recycled sequences, though he was never credited for it.

Director Christy Cabanne and screenwriters Griffin Jay and Maxwell Shane produced the picture. The former had vast experience from the silent era whereas the latter pair were known for their experience working on serials and radio plays. The trio would complement each other, as they would be known in Hollywood circles for working to strict budgets and programs, effectively making them the 'dream-team' of B-movie productions. Their ability to work inexpensively and effectively was never marred in the eyes of the management by their lack of originality, thus ensuring they could churn out relatively cheap and profitable monster flicks for the new management of Universal who after the Laemmles had left were keen to get the company back into the black. There were however, some pluses to this for the audience, namely that the number of productions during this time increased, actors were given slightly more free rein (such as in the comedy or character performances) and the thrills per picture would be prominent and less dramatic, effectively making the pieces escapist and thrilling for audiences at a time of great hardship.

The audience loved the picture, however the critics were not so appreciative of Universal's efforts:

"It's the usual mumbo-jumbo of secret tombs in crumbling temples and salacious old high priests guarding them against the incursions of an archaeological expedition, led this time by Dick Foran, Peggy Moran and Wallace Ford. While the scientists busily explore dank passageways and decipher weird hieroglyphics on tombs and chests, jackals howl outside, the native work-gangs mutiny and the mummy is always just around the corner. Once or twice Miss Moran makes a grimace—as if she had caught an unpleasant odor—and screams. Otherwise every one seems remarkably casual. If they don't seem to worry, why should we? Frightening or funny, take your choice."

Film critic Bosley Crowther, The New York Times

The Mummy's Tomb (1942)

Whereas the original Mummy movie wasn't followed by a sequel but rather a loose remake, this picture would be a sequel to the said remake. The story was wrapped around the premise of a high priest traveling to America with a living mummy to kill those who had desecrated the tomb of an Egyptian princess thirty years earlier. The setting of the movie in modern day America allowed the production to be made cheaply but also gave the audience some welcome familiarity, though technically speaking the picture should be set in the 1970s if it had been thirty years since the previous movie (we, as the filmmakers did, shall glaze over that fact).

"Whether you can believe it or not, the facts are here and we've got to face them. A creature that's been alive for over 3,000 years is in this town."

Universal billed the picture as:

> "The ancient Egyptian Mummy, Kharis, is transported
> from his homeland with the high priest Mehemet (Turhan
> Bey) to wreak vengeance on the family who has defiled
> the sacred tomb of his beloved Princess Ananka.
> Compassionately portrayed by Lon Chaney Jr., Kharis
> travels to the United States, with companion Mehemet, to
> seek archaeologist Stephen A. Banning (Dick Foran).
> Systematically, the last surviving members of the original
> expedition are killed while Mehemet falls in love with
> Isobel Evans (Elyse Knox), Banning's beautiful fiancée. He
> futilely tries to use the Mummy to ensnare Isobel to be his
> high priestess, but is prevented by a fiery mob which
> destroys him and the mummy in this classic chiller."

The appointee of the bandages this time around would be
Universal stalwart Lon Chaney Jr. Chaney, like many of the
incarnations, disliked the makeup for this picture and instead
opted for a rubber mask for as much of the movie as he could be
allowed. The movie was again very much a B-movie after being
allocated a smaller budget than its predecessor, but fans
welcomed it and the critics, who by this time were getting used to
the pattern, were more welcoming than they had been to earlier
pictures from this mold:

> "In 1932 the Mummy was declared to be Boris Karloff; in
> 1940 and "The Mummy's Hand," it was Tom Tyler. Now
> in "The Mummy's Tomb," at the Rialto, it is Lon Chaney
> Jr. Obviously, a couple of these boys are impostors. But
> impostor or not, the present old wrinkle-puss is just as

shriveled of face and as murderous of mind as were his brothers under the skin. Brought in his Mummy's case to a little American town to wreak vengeance upon the family of the archaeologists who profaned Ananka's tomb, he does a pretty thorough job of mayhem and murder before being cremated in a burning mansion while a posse of town's folk watch aghast. But somehow the spell of belief has been broken. The Mummy came to a bad end before, but somehow survived in the person of Mr. Chaney."

The New York Times review from that same year.

Chaney in full Mummy makeup

The Mummy's Ghost (1944)

The next movie from the series would also repeat the pattern of the previous picture by being a direct sequel to its predecessor and would see the return of Chaney. The plot centered on another high priest traveling again to America to reclaim the bodies of an ancient Egyptian princess Ananka and her living guardian mummy, Kharis. Learning that the priest's spirit has been reincarnated into another body, he kidnaps a young woman to aid in bringing her back to life, and all the while his mummy runs amok in modern day America.

Universal billed the picture as:

> "An ancient curse that has survived for 3,000 years is coming to America! In ancient Egypt, the princess Ananka and lowly commoner Kharis fell in love and pledged themselves eternally to each other. Although buried together, Kharis is given a sacred potion that grants him eternal life -- and an eternity to search for his lost love. Lon Chaney, Jr. as Kharis and John Carradine as an Egyptian priest star in this engaging story of a couple's true love that survives the centuries and the unending curse that haunts them. The Mummy's Ghost unearths hope for romantics everywhere with its surprising finale!"

Filming of the picture took just two weeks in the late summer of 1944. The process of making the movie on such a small budget and shooting it so incredibly quickly resulted in two major accidents and two major setbacks. The first was at the beginning of the production where the Amazonian B-movie starlet Acquanetta had been cast into the title role as Mansori. On the very first day on set she was filming a scene where she was due to faint, falling onto what was believed to be a papier-mâché boulder. It was in fact a real boulder and she hit her head and was rushed to hospital. She was treated for concussion and was subsequently released, though badly bruised. Universal, not wanting to wait for her recovery, decided to release her from her contract and instead appoint Ramsay Ames to take on her role. No evidence exists of Acquanetta's initial appointment other than the fact that the costumes that had been made for her did not fit Ames all that well.

Chaney back in the bandages for The Mummy's Ghost

"Now swear by the ancient Egyptian gods, that you will never rest until the Princess Anaka and Kharis have been returned to their rightful resting place, in these tombs..."

The second incident came near the end of production. In a scene that would see the mummy damage the contents of a museum, Chaney, in full makeup (no rubber mask on this occasion) was thrashing about on camera as directed in a sequence that required him to punch his fist through a glass cabinet. Unfortunately, the prop master had not replaced the actual float glass from the earlier shooting with fake, breakaway glass, so instead Chaney smashed his way through real glass. The effect was instant as Chaney can be seen noticeably recoiling from the pain of punching real glass. One shard from the incident flicked out and landed in Chaney's chin (even through his makeup). Chaney subsequently bled but felt okay to continue (such was the tight schedule) and the scene was kept in. The bleeding mummy seen on screen was therefore in fact spouting Chaney's own real blood.

As with its forerunners the picture was welcomed by most, including in this review from the time:

"Bandaged from-head to foot and looking as horrendous as only a Universal property department mummy could look, Lon Chaney is on the prowl again in 'The Mummy's Ghost' at the Rialto. The old boy's bandages are torn and dirty and the spring (what little there was) has gone from his step. He has one good eye, though, and it falls longingly upon the petite person of Amina Mansouri (Ramsay Ames), who actually isn't Amina, etc., at all, but a reincarnation of the Egyptian Princess Ananka, priestess initiate of Arkam, who died accursed three thousand years ago. The lady, it seems, made the mistake of falling in love

with a fellow named Kharis, who was beneath her exalted station. Poor Kharis was buried alive in her tomb as punishment, but every now and then he was permitted a draught of sacred 'tana leave bre'" to keep him 'alive'."

The Mummy's Curse (1944)

"It's as though I were two different people. Sometimes it seems as if I belong to a different world. I find myself in strange surroundings with strange people. I cannot ever seem to find rest!"

Shot a few weeks after The Mummy's Ghost, The Mummy's Curse saw Chaney back in the bandages for the final time. Strangely, the action of the picture had moved from New England to Louisiana, and despite being a sequel the picture focused on a bayou being drained which subsequently lead to a mummy being discovered. The mummy is the same one from the previous film with Princess Ananka also buried within the swamp. The pair are soon awoken and chaos ensues. The movie is relatively unremarkable as it relies heavily on previous footage, stock recordings and the reuse of former sets.

Occasionally mis-billed as The Mummy's Return or The Mummy's Revenge, Universal sought to play up the romance in the flick by putting the word out of this iteration's contents:

"In his last appearance, Lon Chaney, Jr. stars as one of the screen's most memorable movie monsters: the mummy Kharis from ancient Egypt, who is tormented by his

forbidden love for princess Ananka. The trouble begins when mummy Kharis is recovered and transported to Cajun country for study by a bunch of prodding archaeologists. He begins a reign of terror and destruction over the local inhabitants as he renews his search for Ananka's reincarnation. But after the two unite and wreak havoc together, they face a greater threat to their ancient romance than they have ever known -- museums!"

A number of sarcophagi are currently on display in Universal's Prop Department in Hollywood; all of which are available for hire for any prospective productions.

The original working title of the movie was The Mummy's Return as it picks up the action some thirty years after the previous movie. As the previous movies all used the same gimmick of "picking up after thirty years" this picture would have actually have been set in 1997, yet no attempt by the filmmakers was made to set the picture in the future whatsoever.

The movie would also mark the final time the mummy character graced the silver screen from this classic era until 1955's Abbott and Costello Meet the Mummy. Eddie Parker, a mummy stuntman for Curse, was appointed to play the bandaged creep within this comedy flick. The camp monster picture was the last time the mummy was used from this era at Universal until much later, and it also marked the last time that Abbott and Costello worked with Universal producing their "Abbott and Costello Meets" series.

The Mummy (1999)

The manacled mummy of Universal Studios would also return in a new series of movies between 1999 and 2015 with: The Mummy, The Mummy Returns, The Scorpion King, The Mummy: Tomb of the Dragon Emperor, The Scorpion King 2: Rise of a Warrior, The Scorpion King 3: Battle for Redemption and The Scorpion King 4: Quest for Power. Initially planned as a standalone movie, the franchise became one of Universal's most lucrative.

The franchise would take viewers on a journey from the ancient pyramids of Egypt to the Great Wall of China and back. It has had many different cast members, directors and producers throughout its evolution. Although many critics panned its storylines after the first instalment, it still performed well for those who want to see a fun, if fluffy and innocuous, film series. Here are some of the details on each instalment.

It all started in 1999 with The Mummy, which wasn't supposed to be a huge film. In fact, the Universal Studio's budget was only around $10m as they requested a "low-budget horror" film. Producers Sean Daniel and James Jacks took on the project and asked writer Clive Barker to direct it. Clive's vision was a little too dark though, and the studio let go of the project. Soon though George A. Romero, of Night of the Living Dead fame, came into the picture. Romero had his own take on the film, bringing a bit of historical Egypt to the mix. He wanted the story to revolve around Imhotep, who was an Egyptian general alive during the time of Ramesses II and was the same character that Karloff had portrayed years earlier. This story had a very disjointed plotline and the studio was not impressed.

The ill-fated writing of the story kept dragging on. After Barker and Romero left the mix, Joe Dante, Mike Garris and Wes Craven were tapped for inclusion, but for one reason or another they never got involved with the project. Finally, Stephen Sommers contacted Daniel and Jacks and pitched his idea of The Mummy being an updated Indiana Jones-like adventure. He put together an 18-page intro to the story and pitched it to the studio. They finally came on board because of the storyline and even upped the budget to $80m.

Filming began on May 4th of 1998 in Marrakech, Morocco. It moved from there to the town of Erfoud and the Sahara Desert. Finally, it was on to the UK for final shooting in August 1998. Filming was difficult in the desert, however. The Sahara was scorching, and the cast and crew filming there had to drink a special beverage every two hours to avoid dehydration. A spate of sandstorms plagued the area. Spiders and scorpions were a constant threat with more than a few crew members needing airlifting post-bites.

Of the $80m budget, $15m was spent on special effects as created by Industrial Light & Magic. Mummies had to be unique, so as not to be closely identified with other popular mummy movies. The soundtrack was composed by Jerry Goldsmith, with an orchestra led by Alexander Courage. In the end, the film ended up bringing in $260m worldwide. Critics cited it as "good old fun" even if it was vapid on content and storyline. The film and its actors and crew were nominated for a variety of awards including Academy Awards, MTV Movie Awards, Saturn Awards, BAFTA, Sierra and Golden Reel Awards. Of course, its success opened the door for the full franchise to develop.

The Mummy Returns

The Mummy Returns came out in 2001 to a much-awaited anticipation. Due to the success of The Mummy, moviegoers were excited and had high hopes for the sequel. The same actors as the first in the series took up their roles once again. The same production company took the helm as did the director Stephen Sommers.

The storyline starts in 3067BC with the Scorpion King entering the picture. He loses his soul to the Anubis after a deal is made and the Anubis fails to live up to his end of the bargain. Rick and Evelyn O'Connell are exploring a temple in Thebes where they find the Anubis' bracelet. One thing leads to another and the couple are in the mire of Egyptian mummies, curses and scorpions yet again.

At the box-office The Mummy Returns grossed $335m worldwide. On the opening day alone it brought in $24m. Although the critical response was not the greatest, it still earned enough to prove that the franchise was well on its way to mega-success. It earned a slew of nominations including the Saturn Awards for Best Fantasy Film, Best Makeup and Best Special Effects, the Empire Awards for Best British Actress and the Teen Choice Awards for

Choice Actor, Choice Sleazebag and Choice Drama/Action Adventure. It also was the first time the franchise introduced new actor Dwayne 'The Rock' Johnson.

The Scorpion King

Though The Scorpion King was the 2002 release and third in the series of this franchise, it was the prequel to The Mummy Returns. It brought back Dwayne "The Rock" Johnson, Stephen Sommers as producer but with direction by Chuck Russell. It also brought Michael Clarke Duncan into the franchise. This movie takes place 5,000 years ago and tells of The Rock's character Mathayus' beginnings. It tells the story of how he became the Scorpion King.

The storyline and cast veered off from the previous two movies considerably. Critical response was tepid at best, earning moderate reviews from all major name reviewers. The box office however showed a different story. The Scorpion King grossed over $12.5m on its opening day and brought in $36m during the opening weekend. It remained at number one for a few weeks and closed with a domestic gross of over $165m, from a $60m budget. Overall it was a success and led to an assured continuation of the franchise.

The Mummy: Tomb of the Dragon Emperor

The Mummy: Tomb of the Dragon Emperor was released on August 1, 2008. It is considered the third in The Mummy trilogy. Going back to the roots of the franchise, this film brought back Brendan Fraser as the main character and also brought in Jet Li and Maria Bello as co-stars. Rob Cohen directed the film with great enthusiasm stating that he believed it could be better than the first one if the original cast was involved.

Though Cohen didn't get the entire original cast, he did manage to get Fraser, who made the original films exciting and relatable with his modern-day influence. Stephen Sommers, former director of the first two releases, came back, though this time as the producer. What was unique about this film was its departure from its former Egyptian backdrop as it was set and filmed mostly in China.

The idea for this film was taken from real-life Terracotta Army leader Qin emperor Qin Shi Huang. The script was written by Miles Millar and Alfred Gough. Although the film was released in 2008, casting discussions began in 2006. The desire was to get Fraser and Rachel Weisz back to reprise their roles. Fraser confirmed he was on board in 2007 but Weisz declined after just giving birth to her son. Maria Bello was cast as her replacement. The filming for this installment was done in both China and Montreal.

Montreal's Mel's Cite du Cinema was the first destination for photography. It was here that the courtyard scene and the Shangri-la settings were shot. The Terra Cotta mausoleum was also found in Montreal, with 20 different statue heads to be used throughout shots. In October of 2007, filming moved to China. Shanghai Studios was the setting of the 1940s sections of the movie and the chase scenes. A village called Tian Mo was where the general's camp shots were filmed. One downside of filming was the modern-day inconveniences. Filming was done in a real-life training facility that the Chinese army was leasing. It had to be halted frequently when the soldiers had to march the course.

In the end, the movie was released on July 24 of 2008 in Russia and on August 1 of the same year in the US. It ended up grossing more than $401m worldwide. Critics yet again panned the film - even more than other instalments. They claimed a "lack of fun" was the reason for their reviews. Although some good points were featured in reviews, the general consensus was that there weren't enough good points to overcome the bad.

Due to its financial performance, the rumor was that another movie would be put together extending the franchise in this direction. In 2012 however, Universal Studios announced that it had scrapped the plan and instead would work on a reboot with the storyline.

A number of statues and props leftover from these modern Mummy movies are now housed at Universal's huge prop department in Hollywood.

The Scorpion King 2: Rise of a Warrior

The Scorpion King 2: Rise of a Warrior was also released to the movie-going public in 2008, six years after The Scorpion King. This movie had a completely different cast, including a different actor to play the title role. Instead of Dwayne Johnson, Michael Copon took the role of Mathayus.

Filming for this part of the franchise began on October 1, 2007 with a potential release date of August 19 the following year. Originally the name of the film was going to be The Scorpion King: Rise of the Akkadian, however the studio felt that replacing "Akkadian" with "warrior" would be more recognizable for the viewing public. In this movie, a very young Mathayus watches an evil military commander murder his father. His lifelong quest for revenge transforms him into one of the strongest and most feared fighters in the world.

Although in August of 2007 pre-filming it was reported that 'The Rock' would be Mathayus, that was quickly changed when Johnson was unable to fit the filming into his schedule. It also made sense since this version of Mathayus was much younger. It was his young adulthood, so a younger-looking actor was cast in the role.

For the most part the film received negative reviews. It went straight to Blue Ray and DVD. Though it wasn't expected to be a notable success, it still spawned two more films in the sequence.

The Scorpion King 3: Battle for Redemption

The Scorpion King 3: Battle for Redemption again saw a different cast take the lead roles. This time Victor Webster stepped into the role of Mathayus as the central focus of the story. The story follows Mathayus after he becomes The Scorpion King in the previous movie. In this tale, his goal is to protect the Book of the Dead from Talus' hands.

As with its most recent predecessors, it gained negative reactions from critics. The difference with this movie is that it didn't perform at the box office either. It was the second in the franchise that had sales much lower than had been anticipated and hoped for. Critics called it "lacking" and dubbed it the next deterioration of the franchise. Despite its lackluster performance, the fourth installment was still filmed and scheduled for release.

The Scorpion King 4: Quest for Power

The Scorpion King 4: Quest for Power was originally titled The Scorpion King: The Lost Throne. It was released only through Netflix, the first film of the franchise to do so. Again, the cast changed and there was a change of directors and producers, creating a completely different result. Although Victor Webster took on the role of Mathayus again, the remaining cast changed. The addition of Lou Ferrigno, Rutger Hauer and Ellen Hollman made the story completely different. As with the latter movies of the franchise, this one takes place in ancient Egypt and solely follows Mathayus on his journey to find the Urn of Kings.

THE WOLFMAN

"The Count, evidently noticing it, drew back; and with a grim sort of smile, which showed more than he had yet done his protuberant teeth, sat himself down again on his own side of the fireplace. We were both silent for a while; and as I looked towards the window I saw the first dim streak of the coming dawn. There seemed a strange stillness over everything; but as I listened I heard as if from down below in the valley the howling of many wolves. The Count's eyes gleamed, and he said: 'Listen to them the children of the night. What music they make!' Seeing, I suppose, some expression in my face strange to him."

Dracula, Bram Stoker

Werewolves, as with their other monster counterparts, have ancient ancestries. They are a half-breed of man and wolf, often described as standing upright, but still chasing prey on all fours and with a hound's deranged head. Most depictions are powerfully charged with fearsome characteristics of a hunting beast. They are known to howl at the moon ominously and move swiftly over terrain to hunt. It appears that from ancient texts to modern films, art is rife with these mythical creatures.

Where did it all start though? Where did this fictional character come into the mind of writers? Quite possibly the world's fixation on werewolves began with Ovid's Metamorphoses, a book that predates the Bible itself. There aren't werewolves per se as we would know them today, however shape-shifting is a part of the 15-book epic composition. It was the springboard for other writers throughout time who examined the idea of a human taking on different forms, or lycanthropy.

"Then tries to speak, and as he tries he howls;

Still prone to ill, in deeds of slaughter bold,

No more a king, he seeks the shepherd's fold;

His arms are chang'd to legs, the ermin'd pride

That deck'd his form is now a shaggy hide.

Chang'd to a wolf, there still remains behind

Lycaou's manners, and Lycaon's mind;

His hoary locks, his eyc-bal's darling flame,

His savage countenance, are still the same.

But not his race alone is doom'd to fall.

Vice rears her standard o'er the darken'd ball.

From pole to pole the race of man is still

Sworn foe to good, confederate in ill."

Ovid's Metamorphoses 8BC

In approximately 61AD Petronius penned The Satyricon.
Originally in Latin, the book is a combination of prose and verse,
comic and serious writings. The story is told by the main
character, a gladiator named Encolpius, as he travels with two
others - his servant and a companion. At one point they enjoy

dinner at a nobleman's estate, and it is here where table discussions include talk of witches and werewolves. This was evidence of how long people have been discussing werewolves or, in this iteration, the wolf-man. It was discussed as an ancient idea, much like people in the twenty-first century might discuss the Loch Ness monster or Bigfoot. Regardless of the tone, it was more historical evidence that werewolves were prolific throughout history dating back centuries.

> "When I looked around for my companion, he had stripped himself and piled his clothes by the side of the road. My heart was in my mouth, and I sat there while he passed a ring around them and was suddenly turned into a wolf! Now don't think I'm joking, I wouldn't lie for any amount of money, but as I was saying, he commenced to howl after he was turned into a wolf, and ran away into the forest. I didn't know where I was for a minute or two, then I went to his clothes, to pick them up, and damned if they hadn't turned to stone! Was ever anyone nearer dead from fright than me? Then I whipped out my sword and cut every shadow along the road to bits, till I came to the house of my mistress. I looked like a ghost when I went in."

The Satyricon by Petronius

Bisclavret was one of a series of twelve short narratives as penned in the literature of Marie de France (yet again proving that some of the best horror is penned by female authors) in the latter part of the twelfth century. What's different about this contribution is that its main subject is the werewolf. In fact the title Bisclavret means werewolf in French; no longer would the beast be a side story, he would now be the centerpiece. The main character takes the form of a baron who for four days a week lives a normal life, but disappears for the remaining three. His wife finally demands to know where he goes for three days a week and it is here he confides in her, telling her that he is a werewolf. He leaves, hides his clothing, and is a werewolf for his three-day stint. Upon return, he locates his clothing and returns to normal human life.

His wife, upon hearing his secret, decides she does not want anything to do with him and while he is gone, has his clothing hidden from him and marries another man. The werewolf disappears until years later. What is interesting about this piece of classic literature is its focus on the wolf-man character, the ease of shape-shifting back and forth from the two, and the common characteristics of a werewolf. By this time in history, the twelfth century, the werewolf had already been clearly defined as one who is lycanthopic, able to hunt and able to attack at will. This narrative lent its storyline to Old Icelandic tales of the same theme. The Icelandic texts date to approximately the year 1600.

"Since I'm making lais, Bisclavret

Is one I don't want to forget.

In Breton, Bisclavret's the name;

'Garwolf' (werewolf) in Norman means the same.

Long ago you heard the tale told--

And it used to happen, in days of old.

Quite a few men became garwolves,

And set up housekeeping in the woods.

A garwolf is a savage beast,

While the fury's on it, at least:

Eats men, wreaks evil, does no good,

Living and roaming in the deep wood.

Now I'll leave this topic set.

I want to tell you about Bisclavret..."

Bisclavret by Marie de France

Werewolf stories were alive and well throughout the medieval period. Although a single reference was made in The Death of Arthur by Thomas Malory, it was clear that the animal-man character was still a popular subject. In this book, the punishment for betrayal was to turn a man into a werewolf for seven years. An interesting fact to mention with regards to the prevalence of such creatures is the case of Peeter Stubbe, a German man who in the early 1500s was accused, found guilty of, and executed for being a werewolf. It was the first case of its kind, but clear evidence that people believed in the myth. Though it's likely that Stubbe in today's age would have been incarcerated and executed as a serial killer, in those days the story of the werewolf was alive and powerful enough to create a compelling reason for execution. Much of its popularity and acceptance could be attributed to the tales that were handed down through the centuries in both storytelling and literature.

Much later in 1831, Scottish writer Leitch Ritchie penned The Man-Wolf. It is widely credited as one of the first werewolf stories in the annals of British writing. It also features supernatural creatures in addition to the wolf-man. Again, the commonality is the supernatural element to the character. Involved also in the story is a knight, a wife, and a monk who are brave, devious, and cowardly, respectively. By having three main characters from three different personality traits, it gives the reader an introspective of the werewolf from three different perspectives. The knight, for example, views the werewolf as something of a foe that must be vanquished. The wife views it as a creature she wants to manipulate for her own gains. The monk views it as a terrifying character that must be avoided at all costs. If anything, this work was able to convey the total vision of a werewolf throughout history and what it represents.

"At last, amidst the grey mists afar off, between sky and earth, I can just make out a dark speck. The next morning that black spot has grown larger. The Count of Nideck goes to bed with chattering teeth. The next day again we can make out the figure of the old hag; the fierce attacks begin; the count cries out. The day after, the witch is at the foot of the mountain, and the consequence is that the count's jaws are set like a vice; his mouth foams; his eyes turn in his head. Vile creature! Twenty times I have had her within gunshot, and the count has bid me shed no blood."

The Man-Wolf by Leitch Ritchie

A Story of a Weirwolf was written in 1833 by supernatural enthusiast and authority Catherine Crowe. What's interesting about Crowe is that she found a niche market in Victorian culture with her writings and was heralded as a learned resource for the theme of ghosts, lycanthropes and of course, the werewolf. This is a sign of how popular the character had become thanks to writings in classic literature and the short stories of the time. In this story, the setting is Auvergne, France in the sixteenth century. The heroine, Francoise Thilouze, is accused of being a werewolf and of being a witch.

The majestic wolf has inspired writers for millennia

Crowe also penned a novel entitled Light and Darkness; or, Mysteries of Life about fifteen years after A Story of a Weirwolf. In it, she included a chapter entitled "The Lycanthropist." The shape-shifter in this chapter also possessed notable "wolf-like" characteristics and furthered the popularity of the character. It was around this time in the Victorian era where the character's popularity for authors became to expand widely.

Wagner, The Wehr-Wolf is another book that offers up the main character as a man-wolf. In this story, George W. M. Reynolds creates a picture of a 90-year-old man called Fernand Wagner. Wagner makes a deal with the devil to be permanently youthful in exchange for one thing: one day out of every month from that point on, he must become a ferocious werewolf. Of course he accepts the deal and has a wonderful life as a result, except for that one day of the month when he is ravenous to kill. The added feature of this book is that being a werewolf can be advantageous. Wagner, in his human state, commits a crime and is arrested. He turns himself into the monster and escapes. In this instance, becoming the man-wolf creature is a good thing; it allows him to morph and escape.

Although in this story there is an advantage to being a wolf, it also poses its problems when Wagner gets shipwrecked with his love interest Nisida. The two inhabit an island alone and to hide his secret, every month he has to climb to the other side of the mountains to kill on the other side. He is tempted again by the devil to give up his soul for a solution, but declines. They are rescued eventually from the island, and the deal that has become a curse is lifted by a Christian. He then immediately begins aging rapidly and eventually dissolves into a corpse.

This story is interesting in that it explores the werewolf idea from a variety of positions. Yes, it still is a fearsome beast, but it also brings him eternal life. Once he is rid of the form, he is rid of the fountain of youth also, and meets death swiftly. It collects a number of werewolf attributes that had previously been seen in different texts, and starts to form the conventional wolf-man that we know from movies and literature today.

"The usher, awed by the manner of this great functionary, raised the picture in such a way that the judges and the procurator fiscal might obtain a full view of it. A Wehr-Wolf! ejaculated the assistant judge, who had previously remonstrated with his superior; and his countenance became pale as death. The dreadful words were echoed by other tongues in the court; and a panic fear seized on all save the chief judge and Wagner himself. The former smiled contemptuously, the latter had summoned all his courage to aid him to pass through this terrible ordeal without confirming by his conduct the dreadful suspicion which had been excited in respect to him. For, oh! the subject of that picture was indeed awful to contemplate! It had no inscription, but it represented, with the most painful and horrifying fidelity, the writhings and agonizing throes of the human being during the progress of transformation into the lupine monster. The countenance of the unhappy man had already elongated into one of savage and brute-like shape; and so admirably had art counterfeited nature, that the rich garments seemed changed into a rough, shaggy, and wiry skin! The effect produced by that picture was indeed of thrilling and appalling interest! A Wehr-Wolf! had exclaimed one of the assistant judges: and while the voices of several of the male spectators in the body of the court echoed the words mechanically, the ladies gave vent to screams, as they rushed toward the doors of the tribunal. In a few moments that part of the court was entirely cleared."

Wagner, The Wehr-Wolf by George W. M. Reynolds

The 1857 book entitled The Wolf Leader is another piece of literature that is about the wolf-man. The story is the development of a recollection Dumas has from his childhood. In the story, Thibault is a townsman who would command the wolves. In this story, the werewolf again takes center stage. It is further support to the idea that the creatures were considered mystical and powerful. In this tale, the man gets his powers after a one-on-one encounter with a wolf that he bargains with. Despite his heightened werewolf abilities, he still suffers an ill fate, which is common with werewolf characters in history. Though they have powers, they are usually the outcast within a society. Rather than work on relationships with humans, they turn to wolves as comrades, often being able to command them due to being higher in status.

This is another project that included the lycanthropic protagonist who could change into a werewolf. It was written sometime between 1822 and 1860. It is another book in the works of the writing duo of Emile Erckmann and Alexandre Chatrain. Though the text is part of a larger work of many of their writings together, it still is indicative of the longstanding belief in shape-shifting from man to wolf. The duo was famed during their time for penning pieces that normally dealt with the supernatural. They also delved into historical novels, but gained much of their notoriety due to their works of fiction.

What is interesting about another of their stories, Man-Wolf, is that it is an early example of a psychological story. It centers on a strange affiliation between Count Von Nideck and an old witch who is known merely as the "Black Plague." A young doctor is called upon when the Count foams at the mouth, shakes and realizes a wolf-like appearance every year at the same date and time. The interval lasts for about two weeks. At one point, he is found howling and crouching on his knees in his castle. Of course it turns out to be a curse that is lifted once Black Plague dies, but it has a psychological aspect to it in its writing. This is apparent when exploring the situation from the perspective of others living in the castle and how they are toyed with mentally by the annual appearance of the wolf in the Count.

Robert Louis Stevenson's Strange Case of Dr. Jekyll and Mr. Hyde was also a popular novel from the time. Though strictly speaking this isn't a werewolf novel, it deserves a mention due to its lycanthropic nature and its overwhelming popularity. Of course it is Mr. Hyde who is the shape-shifter and accused of many unwanted behaviors. It could be postulated that the shape-shifting feature of the novel was due to various earlier writings on werewolves due to the similarities in attributes. Werewolves are destructive; so was Hyde. Werewolves are able to shift back and forth from man to wolf; Hyde was able to shift from good to bad. Werewolves incite fear in those around them; Hyde was feared by Utterson and other characters. Though Hyde's persona was not defined as a werewolf, he still took on many of the characteristics that they have.

Hector Hugh Munro was known by his pen name Saki. He wrote both The She-Wolf and Gabriel-Ernest in 1910. These stories carried on the tradition of the werewolf. What is interesting about The She-Wolf is that it is a glamorization of unusual powers and esoteric forces. It features Mary Hampton who seemingly first jokes about her houseguest Mr. Bilsiter turning her into a she wolf. Mr Bilsiter immediately shuts down the notion, and Mary postpones further discussion. The commonality of this story and others in history is that the wolf is again regarded as a mystical creature, with one of the characters discussing it as part of "Siberian magic."

Through deception, Mary tricks her houseguests into believing that she turned into a wolf. Some ideas are confirmed about the creature and brought up in their discussion about her changing into the animal. Her houseguests elude to being eaten or attacked by "Mary." This is a sign of how werewolves were perceived: as hunters of prey ready to attack in the night. The guests also discussed fearfully how they might "shut it [the wolf] up" where it can't hurt any person or the animals on the property. Also, Mary is a willing participant who asked to be turned into the creature. When it wasn't possible, she arranged a ruse to fool her guests. She was enticed by the thought of becoming a she-wolf. Though other works in history painted a picture of werewolves as ill-fated creatures, this character was different. She saw becoming the animal as an attractive and exciting alternative to her current form. She had no fear of the animal or its historical reputation; rather, she thought it would be an entertaining joke for her guests to experience.

The other work by Munro was Gabriel-Ernest. In this short story, the main character Gabriel is a werewolf. The story starts to set the stage with the phrases "a wild beast" and "in your woods." The reason for this is to convey that the beast is to be feared and that it runs wild. Both descriptions have a connotation of horror and fear. They conjure up feelings of a ferocious creature roaming through the night in the woods, waiting for a victim. Part of the story leads to Gabriel taking a small child from Sunday school to walk him home. Both disappear though their clothing is found. Neither one is ever seen again.

This carries on the tradition of the werewolf being dangerous. It also juxtaposes the werewolf against Sunday school, or evil and good. By telling a tale of Gabriel leading the child away from school, it's symbolic in stating that going with a werewolf is like being led away from that which is good, or holy. It is the antithesis of both.

"Something had been thinning the game in the woods lately, poultry had been missing from the farms, hares were growing unaccountably scarcer, and complaints had reached him of lambs being carried off bodily from the hills. Was it possible that this wild boy was really hunting the countryside in company with some clever poacher dogs? He had spoken of

hunting 'four-footed' by night, but then, again, he had hinted strangely at no dog caring to come near him, 'especially at night'. It was certainly puzzling. And then, as Van Cheele ran his mind over the various depredations that had been committed during the last month or two, he came suddenly to a dead stop, alike in his walk and his speculations. The child missing from the mill two months ago--the accepted theory was that it had tumbled into the mill-race and been swept away; but the mother had always declared she had heard a shriek on the hill side of the house, in the opposite direction from the water. It was unthinkable, of course, but he wished that the boy had not made that uncanny remark about child-flesh eaten two months ago. Such dreadful things should not be said even in fun."

Gabriel-Ernest by H. H. Munro

The Thing in the Woods was written by Margery Williams Bianco in 1913 and reprinted in 1924. Bianco is best known for her work The Velveteen Rabbit under her unmarried name, Margery Williams. Though this classic written in 1922 was her claim to fame, she was a prolific writer who explored a wide variety of topics and genres before and after The Velveteen Rabbit's publication. The Thing in the Woods is one of her lesser-known works and it featured a werewolf. As is evident in its title, the same fearsome quality was built into this book. It tells the tale of a werewolf and the werewolf's brother, who is closer to human. The two run wild throughout Pennsylvania and wreak havoc on the rural town. The book begins with a fresh-out-of-medical-school physician taking over duties in a small town. After a spate of deaths come in, including the murder of a solo cyclist, the new physician looks to get to the bottom of the crimes. He investigates locations, murdered victims' cadavers and the people in town and it only confirms their notion that a werewolf is the culprit. Throughout the book, the sounds of women screaming in the night can be heard. The townspeople also find men dead with strange markings around their necks that cannot be attributed to any known animals. This books perpetuates the longstanding notion of a creature that hunts humans as prey and is destructive to humans.

The Howling was written in 1977 by Gary Brandner and is perhaps one of the best known and most loved tales of the unbalanced beast. In this novel, Karyn and Roy Beatty are the central characters who move to a quiet village called Drago. Unbeknownst to them, the town is populated by vampires. Karyn is the first one to clue in on something not quite right when she insists she hears howling at night. Her husband is doubtful until he gets bitten one night by a large wolf. That is the beginning of his life as a werewolf. Karyn has to fight to get out of the village. The story keeps the fearsome quality of the creatures and by ganging them together against a helpless woman, it further fuels the idea of innocence being in danger by the creatures. The book was made into a popular movie of the same name in 1981.

Werewolves have worked their way into society and pop culture effectively. Though they are dressed up now as in modern movies and video games, they all hark back to the classic literature from which they were derived. It is there that they were first conjured up in the creative minds of writers and have withstood the test of time.

Werewolf of London (1935)

Long before Lon Chaney Jr. took the shining light of studios in the 1940s it was a different actor and a different movie that began the werewolf fascination for Universal, with 1935's Werewolf of

London. Recognize the name? That's because it has inspired not only the much later John Landis movies of the similar name but also the Warren Zevon hit. Going in back in time to 1913, Universal actually released a short silent movie entitled The Werewolf. Little is known of the picture other than the fact that it was completely lost to time during a fire at the studios in 1927. The picture was mildly successful and was followed up by Universal in 1914 with The Lamb, the Woman, the Wolf, which sometimes appears as The White Wolf. The picture, which was also lost to time, gave the senior Lon Chaney his chance to play the changeable creature. Other studios made similar productions in the 1920s both in the US and Europe, with mixed success. It was however the release of The Werewolf of Paris in 1933 by Guy Endore that really kicked off the wolf-man craze of the middle of twentieth century.

"Sometimes, so my grandmother used to say, men come to the village fair who have never been seen before and never will be seen again. They are men from the sea and are looking for prey to drag down into their underwater dwellings. They can be recognized by the fact that the hems of their clothes are always slightly moist and their hands are often webbed. Their teeth are sharp and pointed. Sometimes they are wolves from the mountains. Then they can be recognized by the hair that grows on the palms of their hands."

The Werewolf of Paris in 1933 by Guy Endore

The novel became a New York Times bestseller within days of its publication. The thriller set across Europe follows Bertrand Caillet as the werewolf, throughout his tumultuous experiences of the

Franco-Prussian War and the Paris Commune of 1870. Despite its success it was rumored that the author, Endore, had sold the manuscript to a publishing house for a flat fee, thus never receiving any royalties. At the time, the effects of the Great Depression were still very evident and although Endore would write a few more novels, they never garnered the success that this book did. Endore ended up working in Hollywood, where initially, it was assumed that he would end up at Universal, as it was the home of horror at the time. This was however not to be, and he was poached by other studios. The year that Werewolf of London came out the author had worked on The Mark of the Vampire and Mad Love for MGM Studios. Universal were not perturbed by this loss of talent and pressed ahead with their own version of the maniacal man-beast.

"With two unsolved murders on their hands, police of Scotland Yard are today working on the theory that the killings have been done by a very prominent man who is suffering from werewolfery, an affliction which changes him into a man-eating beast at night. Fantastic as this may sound, police say they have been in conference with scientists who declare there are two men afflicted in London. An intensive search is now being conducted for the strange man who is believed to be half man and half wolf."

Werewolf of London (1935)

Universal had been working on a script for a wolf-man picture as early as 1932. Keen to capitalize on the successes of the early 1930 monster flicks, they mined libraries and local knowledge bases to find riveting and thrilling tales that they could bring to life. The Laemmles, who were the kings of self-publicity, would informally announce to the public that Lugosi's next epic saga would be that of the lycanthropic beast in late 1932. For various operational reasons and feeling the story wasn't quite how they'd like, the picture was actually shelved until 1934 when a better script was drafted. This new script would become the basis of Werewolf of London. Lugosi would be replaced by Warner Oland due to the former's commitments shooting Mark of the Vampire (1935), with the central role of Wilfred Glendon going to the great stage actor Henry Hull. The plot focused around Dr. Wilfred Glendon's return to London with a rare flower he sought and discovered in Tibet. Unbeknownst to Glendon, he has also been bitten by a werewolf, which causes him to change into one himself during a full moon. Only the juice from his new flower can provide a temporary antidote. However, the flower and Glendon's actions have attracted the attention of the mysterious Dr. Yogami from Tibet (played by Oland).

"Your department is trying to solve two murders. There will be other murders, tonight and tomorrow night – and also next month, when the moon is full again – unless you realize, sir, there is a werewolf abroad in London."

Universal, known for its makeup by this time from the skilled hands of Jack P. Pierce, actually had to tone down the makeup following complaints from the leading actor. Hull, who had been an idol of Broadway for many years, felt that the application of too much makeup by Pierce would mean he wouldn't be able to deliver the performance that he felt the picture needed. Pierce initially resisted the star's complaints and pressed ahead with a rehearsal of the makeup he had extensively designed from his own research into the mystical creature. The actor, complete with makeup, was presented to Universal's management and they declined Pierce's work. Universal said that the combination of the actor's concerns for the part and their own reluctance to enrage the censors meant they could not approve Pierce's designs for the monster and that he should seek to tone down the makeup for the good of the picture. The producers sat down with Pierce and agreed that the picture was about a wolf-man, and that on this occasion there should be more "man" than "wolf." This would make the censors more likely to approve the piece and would surely allow Hull to give the performance he wanted. Pierce was initially furious that his careful design had been rubbished due to the autocratic nature of the industry, but he was consoled about this alteration as in the 1941 version of the movie the producers agreed to use his original makeup design for the werewolf creature.

Universal's first iteration of the maniacal werewolf

"I beg your pardon, sir. I mean, the authorities were gravely concerned with a series of murders, not unlike this one and they were always preceded by the howling of a wolf. And then one night they shot something slinking through the hills and the murders ceased - They said it was a werewolf."

The boundaries and limitations of the censors were tested with the makeup, but it would be the transformation sequence that would prove the sticking point, as it would be the first time such a scene had been made for the cinema. The sequence would in fact be a technical masterpiece that would amaze and delight the audiences of the time. Simply but expertly carried out, the process of Hull's transformation required him to walk along an arcade of columns with the camera seemingly tracking alongside. In essence, this is what happened, but with some very clever editing. Hull would start off at the top of the walkway and would walk to the first pillar, where the shot would be cut. He would then have some makeup applied to make it appear that the transformation was beginning, and would come back and walk to the next pillar. Then there would be another cut, and off to make up he would go before returning slightly more adorned into the transformation. The process would be repeated and then edited together to make the actor appear to be transforming right in front of the audience's eyes; the process was genius. The sequence was the brainchild of cinematographer Charles J. Stumar. Stumar had read up on the character and had directly approached Stuart Walker with the idea. Despite the movie having been in unofficial pre-production for years, the script had only been finalized some two days before production actually started. The hurried nature of the script ensured that vast sequences of unnecessary dialogue were cut out and other sequences changed. Initially, writer John Colton had proposed within this final draft that the transformation sequence should be the actor walking past a large hedge and then emerging on the other side in full makeup. Stumar, who was an old pro within the industry, dreamt up the more sophisticated sequence and thus had it changed to his idea instead. Audiences and critics alike were glad of the change, and many hailed the sequence as the highlight of the picture.

"Werewolfery. Lycanthrophobia is the medical term for the affliction I speak of.

And do you expect me to believe that a man so affected actually becomes a wolf under the influence of the full moon?

No. The werewolf is neither man nor wolf but a satanic creature, with the worst qualities of both."

Werewolf of London (1935)

During production, Carl Laemmle Jr. decided to raise interest in his latest picture by asking studio staff to enter a ballot to come up with a title for the movie. He did this knowing that someone in his huge studio of staff would leak the news to the press and in turn attract free publicity for the film. The ballot asked staff to submit potential titles for the movie, with the winner's title being used on the picture and a $50 cash bonus on their paycheck (which was a considerable sum by 1930s standards). Some of the suggestions submitted were: Moon Doom, Beyond the Ken of Man, Bloom Flower Bloom and The Loose Wolf. The best of the bunch was The Unholy Hour. The ploy worked and articles ran in the local papers. Laemmle picked the winner and paid the worker (rumored to have been a woman working in the costume department). The director however did not like the winning suggestion and the working title of the picture was used instead. Not wanting to go back on his word, the winner's suggestion was used for the Canadian version and some European releases.

Upon release, the picture was widely praised by the critics:

"Designed solely to amaze and horrify, the film goes about its task with commendable thoroughness, sparing no grisly detail and springing from scene to scene with even greater ease than that oft attributed to the daring young aerialist. Granting that the central idea has been used before, the picture still

rates the attention of action-and-horror enthusiasts. It is a fitting valedictory for the old Rialto, which has become melodrama's citadel among Times Square's picture houses."

New York Times review, May 10, 1935

The picture marked a successful return for the studio and Laemmle was keen to have Hull back for more pictures as the leading actor. Hull swiftly declined. He said he enjoyed working on the picture but did not want to end up typecast to this particular genre. Hull would return to the stage before winning parts in a variety of other movies, some of which were with Universal. He would not, however, return to the monster genre. The movie was a mild hit but over the years has been criticized for the lack of humanity in the characters and for the poor script; even the makeup that to many today seems lacking was referenced as being underwhelming. Some critics noted the similarities of the picture with the earlier Dr. Jekyll and Mr. Hyde, which had won an Oscar three years before the release of this movie. However, the movie would soon be pushed aside with the other monster flicks that the Studio was producing with the older, more familiar actors of Karloff and Lugosi, before the beast would return in the 1940s. It is interesting to note that had this movie been a huge success then the story and ethos of the monster we know today would be entirely different. It would be the reboot of 1941 that would finally bring the world the werewolf they had all been waiting for.

The Wolf Man (1941)

"Even a man who is pure in heart

And says his prayers by night

May become a wolf when the wolfs bane blooms

And the autumn moon is bright."

The Wolf Man (1941)

Often billed as the last of the best monster movies released by Universal, The Wolf Man would deliver a powerful addition to the Universal lineup. As iconic as Dracula or Frankenstein's monster, the monster of this movie would grow to become the embodiment of the cinematic werewolf legend. The movie came at a time when Universal had been riding high on the fortunes of the earlier monster flicks. But by 1941 their popularity had waned ever so slightly and a new monster was needed for a new decade to revitalize the box-office returns. Lugosi's star had fallen somewhat by this time, and Karloff by 1941 felt he was perhaps too old to portray the monsters needed, especially with the action required to undertake these parts. Karloff had said that the action sequences of his 1939 rendition of Frankenstein's monster were just too much for his back. It would be a slightly younger actor from a cinematic dynasty with strong Universal ties that would answer the call for a leading monster actor. That actor was Lon Chaney Jr. Before he was considered for the franchise, he had impressed studio heads with his work in the acclaimed Of Mice and Men (1939), and One Million B.C. (1940) before finally slipping into a role more associated with his late father in Man Made Monster (1941). It would be the latter of these (with his role in this horror flick that had been initially written for Karloff) that would finally prove to studio executives that Chaney could easily pull off the role of Larry Talbot for their new werewolf picture.

Where this movie stood out from the rest was its complete presentation of the lycanthropic legend. Building on its predecessor's movie and the literary works of the late Victorian era, this movie would bring together the silver bullet, the change by moonlight and the transformative bite into one package that would delight and inform audiences and filmmakers for generations. The film was seen during production as by no means a classic in the waiting and was given little initial regard. The studio, which was in a pinch after Laemmle's departure, was keen to keep budgets tight in an effort to bring studio expenditure down, and it was for these reasons that the movie was given a B-movie budget. This however, would not stop George Waggner (the director of the piece) from aiming to produce a picture that could equal and rival the monster classics of the preceding decade. Whilst the script was worked on, he assembled an impressive cast of Oscar-nominated and winning actors for the movie, whose working title at the time was The Destiny. Universal was keen to attract Claude Rains to the picture following his earlier successes with the monster franchise. Waggner was pleasantly surprised by this and proceeded to appoint Maria Ouspenskaya who was a highly regarded actress from the time along with other veterans of the backlot, such as Bela Lugosi. Celebrated cinematographer and Oscar nominee Joseph Valentine was hired (he would later go to work on a number of Hitchcock movies). Valentine, like Waggner, shared his view that the picture would take the character in a new direction and for that it would be essential to depict the wolf-man as being on par with the other monsters from the Universal series. This also led to Curt Siodmak coming on board to pen the script. Siodmak, who was a veteran of the old German noir and gothic film industry, was right at home working on this picture. His talents for the gothic were highly appreciated as he wove a tale of action, adventure and suspense in a rich and well-conceived plot that used the ancient legends to present a relevant and deeply entertaining flick. It was also he who in invented the werewolf poem (and the silver bullets plot device) that have been seen numerous times in movies and novels ever since.

"Doctor Lloyd: I believe a man lost in the mazes of his own mind may imagine that he's anything."

As with many of the other movies, the picture was shot entirely on the expansive Universal backlot, with the European sets and the Court of Miracles in particular being the scene for most of the action. The film makers decided to not tie themselves to any fixed moment in time by creating an exact setting for the movie, as this had plagued some of the latter Mummy movies. Instead a vaguely Anglo-European type village was used with the timeline of the movie being set in roughly the present day but without the real-world irks of the then World War (the churchyard and cathedral scenes, for example, were used in The Hunchback of Notre Dame where Chaney's father had played Quasimodo back in 1923). In real-time, the war was raging in Europe and other territories. The photography took place in November 1941, and production wrapped a few days before the attack on Pearl Harbor in December of that year which brought the US into the worldwide conflict. In the picture though, the escapist feel of the movie ensured that no real-world problems such as this would distract the audience's attention. This is why a heavy emphasis is placed on the opening credits and throughout the movie to inform the audience that this is a legend and tale at best; it was something to enjoy and to distract audiences from the horrors that were rampant at the time of the release.

"Sir John Talbot: Yes, that's the sign of the werewolf.

Larry Talbot: That's just a legend though, isn't it?

Sir John Talbot: Yes, but like most legends, it must have some basis in fact. It's probably an ancient explanation of the dual personality in each of us."

The plot can be summarized thus: Larry Talbot (Chaney), having spent 18 years in the US, returns to his ancestral home in Europe. While staying with his father and trying to make amends with him, he meets an array of new people within the grounds and village. Larry expresses his sorrow over the death of his older brother, the heir to the family estate, John. Events take a turn for the worse when he is bitten by a werewolf and becomes one himself, befalling the same fate as his dead brother. Transformed by the full moon, Larry heads for the forest and a series of events occur. Siodmak would later credit his experiences of fleeing the Nazis in the 1930s as his inspiration for many of the scenes in the movie. The normal and carefree life descending into sheer terror and chaos when the Nazis took control of Germany can be seen as a key likeness to the Talbot character. Likewise, the wolf-man and his heinous acts can be seen as a metaphor for how the Nazis had transformed Europe at the time.

Lugosi had a central role within the story, as the gypsy who tells Talbot his fortune before turning into a wolf and biting Talbot to unleash the events that follow. The wolf that he turns into was in fact a German shepherd dog named "Moose" who was owned by one of the production crew. Lugosi gives a solid supporting actor performance, now comfortable in the genre that he had helped to create in the previous decade. Similarly, Rains and the other cast all use the rich script to elevate the picture above its B-movie production budget.

Whereas Werewolf of London had portrayed a rather ingenious method of transformation for the title character, the studio heads at Universal had given the director an emphatic "no" to the creation of such a scene in this film – purely for budgetary reasons. This decision would inform Siodmak's script from the outset as he would choose to add more suspense (which remained) and to use a plot device that depicts Talbot as someone who was unsure as to whether he was actually the wolf-man. This ambiguous positioning would see the creature never appearing on screen.

Waggner felt they would be hard-changing the audience if they did not deliver a monster to shock them within the movie, and that leaving it all mysterious and unseen would not be deliverable to audiences that demanded a monster in their monster movies. Waggner argued with the executives that bad reviews would be attracted that would negatively affect the movie's performance at the box-office if no monster was seen on screen. It would be this financial reasoning that hit home with the powers that be and ensured that the transformation and the monster itself would be seen on screen. The script was subsequently revised and the budget increased to support this decision. It was at this juncture that the idea to reuse Pierce's unused designs for the makeup were put back into the production program.

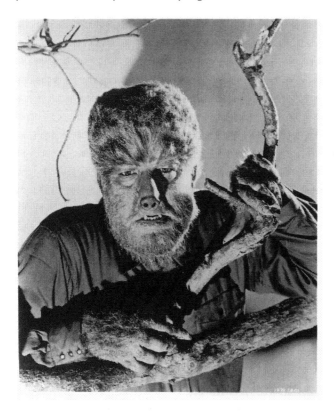

Chaney in full werewolf makeup

"Maleva: Whoever is bitten by a werewolf and lives becomes a werewolf himself.

Larry Talbot: Ah, don't hand me that. You're just wasting your time.

Maleva: The wolf bit you, didn't he?

Larry Talbot: Yeah. Yes he did!"

As with all B-movie productions (though one could argue the movie was at least an A-minus-movie!), the production was rapid with the photography taking a mere few weeks to fully shoot. The production was not without its setbacks though. Actress Evelyn Ankers complained to the producers several times about Chaney's penchant for scaring her while on set. The makeup would take over six hours to apply and three hours to remove. Pierce would use a combination of yak hair, spirit gum and cotton balls to create the iconic look, sometimes spending even more hours in redressing the facial makeup when not worn, in order to make it last the production and stay consistent. This meant that Chaney spent hours just wandering the lot in full makeup waiting for scenes to be set up. Ankers would also have further reason to complain when a bear that was drafted in to wrestle the wolf-man in the forest broke loose from his chains and chased the poor actress up onto a catwalk high above one of the soundstages. The scene was subsequently edited out of the final movie, though snippets of it can be seen in the official trailer released at the time. She would also suffer another issue when filming the final fight scene. In the sequence she faints and basically sits out the whole climatic event. However, unbeknownst to Universal she did act as if she was faint but then subsequently <u>did</u> actually faint during the filming. While the fight was shot, the scene had low-level fog pumped into the area to give some dynamic drama to the sequence; the fog would actually cause Ankers to lose consciousness. After the scene was shot, the crew began to set up for the next scene, not noticing that Ankers was still in the same position. Some moments passed before they realized she wasn't acting in method but had actually become overwhelmed from the chemical fog and would need to be revived. She would later recount that the filming of this picture was one of the worst professional experiences of her life.

The movie was well received by critics and audiences alike. Variety reported:

> "The English legendary werewolf provides basis for another cinematic adventure into the horrific chiller-diller realm. The Wolf Man is a compactly-knit tale of its kind, with good direction and performances by an above par assemblage of players, but dubious entertainment."

The New York Times was equally impressed:

> "Universal, which must have a veritable menagerie of mythological monsters, all with an eye on stardom and a five-year contract, is now sponsoring the debut of its latest pride and joy, 'The Wolf Man' at the Rialto. Perhaps in deference to a Grade-B budget it has tried to make a little go a long way, and it has concealed most of that little in a deep layer of fog. And out of that fog, from time to time, Lon Chaney Jr. appears vaguely, bays hungrily, and skips back into mufti. Offhand, though we never did get a really good look, we'd say that most of the budget was spent on Mr. Chaney's face, which is rather terrifying, resembling as it does a sort of Mr. Hyde badly in need of a shave. Privately, and on the evidence here offered, we still suspect that the werewolf is just a myth."

The cast and crew's ambitions to present an A-movie on a B-movie budget were successful and it helped catapult the wolf-man to the level of Dracula, Frankenstein's Monster and The Mummy. It was hugely successful at the box-office and ensured that Universal stayed in the monster-making business for years to come, but more importantly it defined the genre and set the bar for later movies. It ensured that the older performers and crew could be led into a new generation of pictures and it made a star of Lon Chaney Jr., no longer living in the shadow of his father's work. The movie was an all-round success and Universal could not be happier.

Frankenstein Meets the Wolf Man (1943)

The second wolf-man picture or fifth Frankenstein film - I'll let you take your pick - would be one of the first crossovers of the monster movie franchise in Universal's history. The fifth Frankenstein movie would see the character become intertwined with the Wolf Man franchise. This would be released in 1943 and would again star Bela Lugosi but this time, finally, as the Monster. The movie would act as sequel to the original Wolfman movie and as the star of such, Lon Chaney Jr. had to swop from the platform boots to the hairy costume. This would necessitate Lugosi's portrayal of the character, some 12 years after he was originally attached to play the Monster.

It started with Curt Siodmak who, fresh from the success of writing the first Wolfman movie, was sitting in Universal's commissary on the lot one day in 1942 when he joked to George Waggner that he had created a new idea for the monster series of Frankenstein Meets the Wolf Man. He explained a bit about it, said that he would do anything right now as he needed money to buy a new car and then purposely mispronounced the name as "Frankenstein Wolfs the Meat Man." Waggner, not known for his sense of humor, got up from the table and left. A few hours later, Waggner called Siodmak in his office. The phone rang and Waggner said in a dry voice "go buy your car." Shocked by Waggner's seriousness, within days Siodmak had been appointed to draft the full script and within a month had bought himself the new car he had desperately needed. The movie would be called Frankenstein Meets the Wolf Man and would serve as a sequel to the highly popular The Wolf Man movie and The Ghost of Frankenstein.

"Lawrence Talbot: You think I'm insane. You think I don't know what I'm talking about. Well you just look in that grave where Lawrence Talbot is supposed to be buried and see if you find a body in it!"

The story would follow on from the last Wolf Man movie where Talbot's grave now opened on a full moon night has caused him to rise again (making him, in the subsequent films, technically one of the undead). The full moon, which had not been mentioned in the first Wolf Man movie, is now explained in this picture as the cause of the resurrection of the character. Universal does this by changing the last section of the infamous poem to read "...and the moon is full and bright," thus letting the audience know that it is the moon that causes him to change. Later our protagonist Talbot is locked away in an asylum following an operation that he had endured to fix his transformative problem. An inspector visits him to question him about a spate of murders that have occurred recently. Talbot soon escapes and meets up with a gypsy. The gypsy, knowing of his condition, takes him to the only man that she knows who could fix him, Dr. Frankenstein. They later discover that the doctor is long dead but they do locate his daughter. Talbot begs the daughter for her father's notebooks and texts detailing the secrets of life and death. She doesn't have them, so together they travel to his former castle to locate the works. There they come into contact with the Monster and all chaos breaks loose.

The setting for the movie and the location of the castle would be clearly defined within the picture, even though the locations of such were either unclear or more Germanic in location, particularly the latter for the earlier Frankenstein movies. The country would be the fictional "Vasaria" and not Germany or any other known European state. The producers made this decision as the picture was made during World War Two and they did not want any connection between the atrocities that were occurring in mainland Europe and the contents of the movie. Incidentally, the word "vasaria" means "place of water" in German, which connects the uses of the dam, waterfall and hydroelectric turbine that are seen in the movie.

Karloff, who had been wary of playing the brutish monster, was not selected and instead Bela Lugosi was approached. Lugosi who was top of the pile for monster movies at the time quickly became the producers' first choice. However, Lugosi was not interested in playing the non-speaking murdering dummy at all. Waggner would actually leave the production midway through pre-production to work on other projects, and it was this change in direction for the picture, with heavy script revisions, that finally enabled Lugosi to take on the part. Initially, Siodmak had proposed that Lon Chaney Jr. play both monster parts as he had experience of both. However, fearing the potential time overruns for swopping makeup they decided against it and cast Lugosi (who actually celebrated his 60th birthday while shooting this movie).

"Lawrence Talbot: Why have you followed me?

Dr. Frank Mannering: Talbot, you're a murderer.

Lawrence Talbot: Prove it.

Dr. Frank Mannering: You're insane at times and you know it. You're sane enough now though to know what you're doing.

Why don't you let me take care of you?

Lawrence Talbot: You think it would do any good to put me in a lunatic asylum?

Dr. Frank Mannering: You know that's where you belong. It's the only thing to do.

Lawrence Talbot: Oh that wouldn't do any good. I'd only escape again sooner or later.

Dr. Frank Mannering: We might be able to cure you. It might prevent you...

Lawrence Talbot: I only want to die. That's why I'm here. If I ever find peace I'll find it here."

Lugosi accepted the role based on the fact that the Monster had a rather large speaking part throughout the movie, where he would talk about the events of the last movie and his fears of going blind (a side-effect from the transplant that occurred in last movie). The manner in which he would walk was also discussed as the straight-armed lunge walk was first thought to express his poor vision, a connotation that is now iconic for the Monster's trademark walk. Siodmak said that he had drafted some interesting dialogue for the creature to emphasize the pain and agony of the assembled fiend. Producers weren't so sure about the move. Instead, they filmed a number of sequences and brought test audiences in to a small screening to gauge public opinion. Supposedly, the test was negative and the public thought the monster more comical than scary from this showing.

Instead, the producers decided that the monster must remain nearly mute for the duration of the movie. In an effort not to enrage their main star, they made the movie with Lugosi believing it was a speaking part. On completion they edited out all of the

Monster's speaking scenes with the exception of two sequences where his mouth can be seen opening but his voice had been dubbed out. All references to the Monster's blindness were also cut due to the fact that it was the Monster who described his pain of losing his sight and with his dialogue now cut they could not bring the condition into the picture. The shuffling and stiff-armed walk were all now motiveless, with members of the public merely believing that Lugosi had created these attributes to make his mark on the character. Therefore, as the Monster was heavily cut out of the picture, it is the Wolf Man who stars in most of the picture, making this movie more of sequel to his franchise of movies.

Lugosi as the Monster with Chaney's Lawrence Talbot

Lugosi, by this time had been suffering from exhaustion. The actor who had most famously played Count Dracula had been constantly busy with films and productions ever since his big screen debut, and by the production of this movie and his significant birthday halfway through he had become weary and the need for stand-ins was deployed heavily. Though not credited, Gil Perkins, the production's main stunt double would fill in for Lugosi for lighting tests and even for some of the earlier scenes now cut from the production. One scene where the Monster is seen buried in ice was in fact Perkins and not Lugosi. Strangely, Eddie Parker who was billed as Lugosi's stand-in and stunt performer was believed to have undertaken more of the Wolf Man's stunts, though in at least one shot he dons the green makeup to play the monster in both Lugosi's and Perkins' respective absences. The side effect of having three actors play the role of the Monster does hinder Lugosi's portrayal and characterization of the character, and it also leads to a number of continuity issues. These were made worse by the rushed final editing undertaken to reduce the Monster's sequences.

Reviews were positive, though, with Variety in particular being especially positive about the monster mash up:

> "In order to put the Wolf Man and the Monster through further film adventures, scripter Curt Siodmak has to resurrect the former from a tomb, and the Frankenstein creation from the ruins of the castle where he was purportedly killed. But he delivers a good job of fantastic writing to weave the necessary thriller ingredients into the piece, and finally brings the two legendary characters together for a battle climax."

Not everybody was happy with the movie though. The New York Times was quite "disappointed" in the picture; they and fans argued that the actual fight between the monster came too little and too late into the picture. Others argued that with a few tweaks and a bit more action, Universal could be "onto something" with the crossing over of their franchises. Others praised the movies suspense and pacing, in an effort that engages and keeps the audience's attention throughout. Whatever the opinion and however divided it was, it would set the standard for these crossover movies. The first of its kind, it would inspire not only Universal but other filmmakers too. In later years, similar franchises that may or may not be owned by the same company started to use the technique to draw fans and audiences together. Sci-fi/horror examples include: Alien vs. Predator, Freddy vs. Jason and the 1962 film King Kong vs. Godzilla (in fact this movie would be honored in the former two by being played in the background in some of the scenes). Other lesser thought- of examples would be in the cartoon world with Scooby Doo and Who Framed Roger Rabbit? or in the action and adventure arena with the Marvel Cinematic Universe. This movie spawned this idea, and for that we must be grateful to Curt Siodmak and his desperate need to buy a new car.

Sequels

Unfortunately for the Wolf Man, unlike the other creatures in the Universal monster catalogue he would not be given his own outright sequel; instead, due to the popularity of the previous movie the order of the day would be the mashes of different franchises that seemed to set the box-offices alight.   In House of Frankenstein (1944), Talbot is once again brought back to life and is promised a cure via a brain transplant, but is instead shot dead with a silver bullet. He would return in House of Dracula (1945), where he is finally cured of his condition. Without explanation he is then strangely afflicted once more, in the comedy film Abbott and Costello Meet Frankenstein (1948). This time the Wolf Man is a hero of sorts, saving Costello from having his brain transplanted by Dracula (Bela Lugosi) into the head of the Monster (now played by Glenn Strange). Talbot fights Dracula as he turns into a bat, he then dives over a balcony into the sea, taking Dracula with him. The trio of monsters were never seen again after this point in the classical era.

House of Frankenstein (1944)

Whereas Frankenstein Meets the Wolf Man had been the first pairing or "versus" movie of its kind, it would be House of Frankenstein where the first multi-monster combination would be deployed. Early drafts of the picture by Siodmak had included far more monsters than seen on screen, including: the Mummy, the Ape Woman, the Mad Ghoul, and the Invisible Man. However, due to the fast-paced nature of the production there had not been time to assemble as many actors and crew as were needed to pull-off such a task. The working title of the picture, Chamber of Horrors (later changed to The Devil's Brood) suggests this move from the outset.

"Dr. Gustav Niemann: Fifteen thousand Marks. A thousand for every year I spent in a stinking, slimy dungeon. You bargain poorly, Herr Ulman.

Ullman: Don't kill me!

Dr. Gustav Niemann: Kill my trusted old assistant? Why, no. I'm going to repay you for betraying me; I'm going to give that brain of yours a new home in the skull of the Frankenstein monster. As for you Strauss, I'm going to give you the brain of the wolfman so that all your waking hours will be spent in untold agony awaiting the full of the moon... which will change you into a werewolf."

The movie would be the first time that Glenn Strange played the Monster. Karloff who had been cast as the mad scientist of the piece, actively coached Strange in order for him to pull off the character in the way that he had portrayed the brute. It would also mark Karloff's final performance in the Universal's classic horror cycle.

The plot was simplistic but the real motives of the picture would be showcasing the monsters within. After escaping from an asylum the mad Dr. Niemann (Karloff) and his hunchback assistant revive Count Dracula, the Wolf Man and Frankenstein's Monster in order to exact revenge upon a number of the doctor's enemies.

The movie was mildly successful at the box-office with critics such as the New York Times stating that the movie relies heavily on the tongue-in-cheek nature of the piece and that Universal were in danger of making a pastiche of their popular franchise:

> "Universal, generous to a fault, has presented as complete a gallery of ghouls as ever haunted a Hollywood set in "House of Frankenstein," the horror spectacle which arrived at the Rialto yesterday. A necrology of the inmates of this macabre manse includes practically everyone in Universal's vicious varsity from Dracula to that eminent werewolf, Lon Chaney. It's like a baseball team with nine Babe Ruths, only this grisly congress doesn't hit hard; it merely has speed and a change of pace. As such, then, it is bound to garner as many chuckles as it does chills. However, lampoon or no, put this item down as a bargain for the bogie hunters."

House of Dracula (1945)

It would be the House of Dracula that finally made the first and final true crossover of monster characters. Whereas Dracula had been separate and somewhat distant in the previous installation, he would take center stage in this production. The working titles for the movie were reported as Dracula vs. the Wolf Man or The Wolf Man vs. Dracula. It would also see one actor portray the characters of the Monster and Wolf Man. Chaney, who had top billing for the film, played the Wolf Man for the entirety of the picture and filled in for Strange's Monster in just one sequence. There would, though, be a recycling of footage to keep costs down where both Chaney's Monster from The Ghost of Frankenstein and Karloff's from The Bride of Frankenstein would be used, along with Eddie Parker who played the Monster in the fire scene towards the end. Chaney did not really play both creatures until the comedic follow-up Abbott and Costello Meet Frankenstein in 1948.

The plot focused around Dracula, with his Machiavellian methods being the main drive of the picture. Dracula arrives at the doctor's office seeking a cure for his vampirism. However, this is a ruse by Dracula to turn the doctor's assistant into a vampire. Meanwhile, a more sincere Talbot arrives at the same place seeking a cure for his lycanthropy. When the doctor's first attempt fails, Talbot tries to commit suicide by jumping off a cliff, but instead finds a network of underground caves where Frankenstein's Monster is in stasis from the previous picture. The monsters then battle for supremacy.

"Dr. Edelman: What are you doing here? Who are you?

Count Dracula: I am Baron Latos. I have come to you for help.

Dr. Edelman: It's five o'clock in the morning.

Count Dracula: I must apologize for the intrusion. But travel is very difficult for me, and I've come a long way.

Dr. Edelman: I don't understand.

Count Dracula: Perhaps you will, after you've led me to the basement room of this castle.

Dr. Edelman: Eh - a very strange request. This castle is my home!

Count Dracula: Have no fear, doctor. Had conditions permitted, I would have presented myself in the usual manner.

Dr. Edelman: Well, it is most unusual...

Count Dracula: I will explain everything, before sunrise."

The very first script of the movie was rejected by the censors as being too graphic and too violent. The movie's script was then revised to tone this down. Initially, the script had been written as The Wolf Man vs. Dracula as a proposed direct sequel to the more popular Frankenstein Meets the Wolf Man. However, the main sequence that was objectionable was seeing the Wolf Man do battle with a giant bat (as Dracula) that would see the pair fighting whilst the villagers gathered around to spectate. The sequence would end with the villagers attacking the pair during the fight and burning down the house. The Wolf Man was supposedly meant to react to this with a mass-killing of a number of villagers. Instead, all of this was toned down to the slightly tamer version that we now know.

"Lawrence Talbot: Get out! It's the Frankenstein monster!"

Strange recounted years later that the movie was not without it setbacks during the production. He recalled that one scene where the Monster is stuck in quicksand was particularly difficult to film. He said that he would be in full makeup, which itself would take four hours to apply successfully, he would then be dunked into this tank of wet sand to be filmed all day. Instead of taking him out during set changes or rig movements, they just left him in there all day. As a result, he was freezing by the end of the day. Chaney who was no stranger to working on sets that required a lot of technical adjustment would sympathize with his colleague by passing him his whiskey to drink between takes in an effort to keep him warm. The result would be that by the time they had fished him out of the tank by the end of the day, he was completely drunk. The process of then removing his makeup, followed by putting on his normal clothes became a complex one. Chaney, who would also end up most days by drinking, started to show the signs of alcoholism. For this reason, at the end of the 1940s he would be let go by Universal.

Reception of the movie was tepid at best with Variety reporting:

> "Universal has brought all of its terror figures - Dracula, the Wolf-man and Frankenstein's Monster - together in a nifty thriller for the chiller trade."

The movie would ultimately be the seventh to feature the Frankenstein monster but by this point he is relegated to just a bumbling servant to the other, wiser characters. The movie also borrows heavily from past movies and even recycles footage along with dialogue; the tried and tested formula by this point was incredibly stale. The movie is not however without its good points. The performance of Chaney in his Wolf Man role was as good as his original performance, particularly in the scenes where he plays the tormented Talbot, now finally "cured" of his condition and able to walk freely in the moonlight. It would also be the final time that Jack Pierce would work on a Universal monsters picture, having been let go from Universal some months after the production wrapped. Pierce's more authentic grease paint and spirit gum would be replaced with cheaper and timelier latex coverings as applied by his successor Bud Westmore.

It might have been the reduction in the script's quality following its heavy revision or Universal's own tight grip on the budget, but whatever the reason, the movie was very much in the B-movie category when compared to other entries in the series. This last proper monster movie (before they descended into farce) was not taken lightly by the cast and crew. Despite the tight budget, all the assembled cast took the movie wholly seriously and set out to make a swansong that many (including Chaney and Pierce) must have known would be one of their last together, especially as Karloff and Lugosi were also coming to an end of their time on these classic monster movies. The movie should have had a larger budget to match the ambition of the filmmakers but alas it was not meant to be. This meant that the final installation of the monster franchise is a little lackluster in places, though overall it does prove itself by delivering the goods that you would expect. The movie, on reflection, would mark the end of the popular classic monster pictures.

> "The Frankenstein monster! That must be the skeleton of Dr. Niemann who revitalized him years ago. As the story goes, the villagers drove them into the swamp and they went down in the quicksand. After all these years, the mud has brought them here. He's still alive. He's indestructible. Frankenstein's creation is man's challenge to the laws of life and death!"

The Wolfman (2010)

> "Even a man who is pure in heart and says his prayers by night, may become a wolf when the wolfbane blooms, and the autumn moon is bright."

Though the Wolfman did not have any direct sequels for his own franchise, he did have a modern day retelling in The Wolfman (2010). The plot would largely follow the original movie which sees Lawrence Talbot as he returns to his childhood home of

Blackmoor after the death of his brother. The rumor is that his brother was killed by a feared werewolf running wild in the town. Featured in the 2010 version are Anthony Hopkins, Benicio Del Toto, Hugo Weaving, Emily Blunt and Geraldine Chaplin. Rick Baker created The Wolfman's special effects with David Self and Andrew Kevin Walker penning the script.

Production for the film began in March 2006 when Universal Studios announced that they were re-imaging The Wolf Man from 1941. Writer Andrew Kevin Walker was tasked with developing the plot and creating additional characters to carry the story. He also was able to use modern technology and visual effects to develop the storyline beyond its predecessor.

Originally, critically-acclaimed director Mark Romanek was tied to the picture, however due to creative differences, he ended up bowing out of the project. Universal Studios embarked on a search to find the right person to direct. They considered names such as James Marigold, Frank Darabont and Brett Ratner, among others. In the end, they chose John Johnson. He hired David Self to work with Andrew Kevin Walker on the script's rewriting.

> "It was about twenty-five years ago now. My pa found him: Quinn Noddy and all his flock. Brains, guts and God-knows-what lying across the moor. And the look on Quinn's face. Like he'd been eaten alive. Whatever did it, it was big, had claws, and didn't mind a load of buckshot. After that, me father went home. He melted down my ma's wedding spoons, and cast silver bullets off 'em. He wouldn't leave the house on a full moon from then on."

From March 3 to June 23 of 2008, filming took place in Britain. Locations included Castle Combe in Wiltshire and Derbyshire. The stately home Chatsworth House was transformed into the dark and overgrown area needed by adding ivy, dead grass and weeds to its then-green landscape. Stowe House in Stowe, Buckinghamshire, was used for a morbid funeral scene. The initial budget for the picture was $85m.

Rick Baker was the creator of the makeup used for the main Wolfman character. He and Del Toro agreed that staying true to the original Wolf Man from 1941 was key to successful characterization. Johnson chose one of Baker's early renderings as the design to be used for makeup. In the end, makeup took three hours to apply to Del Toro's face every day and one hour to remove. They used loose hair and latex prosthetics, along with wigs and dentures. They knew that computers would be used to transform Del Toro into the Wolfman, which was a sticking point for Baker who believes realism would not be achieved. Due to time limitations, however, they were forced to proceed as planned.

The goal was to shoot Del Toro as a man and then as the Wolfman. They would go back during post-production to decide on the second-by-second transformation and how it would play out in the final version. This was the main reason for using CG technology.

In May of 2009 the first reshoot was held in Greenwich on the grounds of the Old Royal Naval College. In this portion of production, changes were made and a scene was added. First of all, the werewolf was changed to run on all fours, rather than standing on two legs. Second, a scene was added with the Wolfman and the werewolf. These additions extended the delivery date; a common plague for the film from the beginning.

Director Johnson originally stated he could finish filming in 80 days. That target was never achieved due to consistent problems with reshoots, rewrites, re-edits, and changes to the music. The film was originally set for release in November of 2008 but didn't make it to the big screen until February of 2010. Release dates came and went, with Universal Studios making periodic announcements about its official release. Though originally it was expected in November of 2008, the first postponement put its release date to February of 2009. In April of that year, however, it was moved to November. It was moved again to July of 2009. Its first official promotion began as its trailer was released on August 21, 2009 during the film Inglourious Basterds. The movie would finally be released at the premier in Rome in January of 2010 and in the rest of Europe the following month.

Benicio del Toro in full makeup for the movie

Opening weekend saw revenues of over $31m worldwide, coming in second for the weekend behind Valentine's Day. After its full run, it ended up grossing $61m in North America and totaled $139m throughout the whole world. The production cost, however, was $150m, which made it a box office flop. Studio president Ronald Meyer stated that he was very unhappy with the finished product and was annoyed that it did not make back the massive investment the studio had placed on it.

Critical reviews were just as negative, with about 70% of critics citing major problems with the film. What saved much of the film was its cinematography. The sweeping visuals and large-scale efforts to create true-to-period backdrops were not without merit. Locations were used well, according to critics, to build a grand landscape in which the Wolfman romped; it effectively showcased his tortured soul and the troubles of those around him.

The major problem and reason for negative reviews was the CGI effects when transforming Del Toro into the Wolfman. Though the makeup was considered excellent, as evidenced by the movie winning "Best Makeup" at the Saturn Awards, it was the transition from man to wolf that was notably rough. Many said that if Baker had got his way and allowed for the movie to be made with less CGI then perhaps the final cut may have been much better. There was one small glimmer of hope for the movie that came even before it was released.

Located inside Soundstage 22 at Universal Orlando's Halloween Horror Nights was perhaps (at the time) one of the most immersive houses they had ever built. The house had been designed with the co-operation of the Universal production staff who were working on the movie while the house was being built. The aim was for guests to experience the movie and then experience the house. However, due to production setbacks, the movie's release date was delayed until after the event, and so the new ethos became, "Enjoy the house and then enjoy the movie." (Guests had to wait until January 2010 to enjoy the movie.) Despite this timing issue, the house was exceedingly impressive.

Guests first encounter a gypsy settlement where the gypsies tell foreboding stories about "the beast" before being led into the forest. This was one of the most detailed scenes ever created at Universal, with guests staring in wonder at the immersive detail that included real trees, moss, grass, hills, fog, gravel, and even a "moon," combined with the sound of pounding feet as the mysterious beast drew closer and closer before an inexplicable howl rang out. Guests could be forgiven for thinking that they had teleported to the Scottish moors. James-Michael Roddy told the Orlando Sentinel at the time:

> "We were basically given access to all their [the film producer's] designs, and this is a big-budget version. A lot of amazing production value has gone into it. Although the house is built inside a soundstage, it has an outdoors feel with a gypsy camp, a forest and the sensation of being chased by a lycanthrope. This is the only place you're going to be able to see the Wolfman [at the time]. It doesn't open until February (sic), so that's pretty cool for us."

After exploring the moors, guests enter the village, the mansion, and the crypt from the movie, before the beast begins to actively target them. Eventually, they're led back into the woods (a different scene) with the Wolfman in pursuit, jumping between hills and hedges as he chases the intruders to his domain (scareactors were literally flying overhead). Finally, guests reach a mound where the Wolfman jumps onto a large, natural plinth to howl at the moon above. As guests stare in fright and wonder what happens next, a hunter emerges from the side, armed with a blunderbuss loaded with a silver bullets and fires at the beast, sending the scareactor tumbling down the hill below. Guests make their final run for the exit, as the angry Wolfman would appear to launch one final attack and for them to receive one final scare.

The Wolfman character would also be celebrated that year as an icon for the Halloween Horror Nights event, which afforded him the opportunity to appear in the commercial that appeared around the States in late 2009. From within it he would be seen in the lobby of the Universal Palace Theater. When a movie patron enters the lobby to buy refreshments, Wolfman growls at the unsuspecting customer before launching to attack him.

The 2010 remake film was by many accounts a failure. It didn't meet financial expectations. It lost millions of dollars. The critics sadly panned it. Still, the cinematography and actor's performances were noted as excellent. The house, too, at Halloween Horror Nights was excellent. Although it was positive in many respects, it will still go down in cinema history as a lost opportunity to portray the legendary Wolfman. It is with high hopes that we now wait for a new movie from this franchise to appear in 2018.

"Terrible things, Lawrence. You've done terrible things!"

THE INVISIBLE MAN

Technological background

The Victorian era (1837 to 1900) was a time of many changes and developments in technology. Those changes were incorporated into writings of science fiction released in the era. One by one, great novels were created and their backdrop was the changes the world was going through. The world was still coming to terms with Darwin's Origin of Species (published 1859) and it seemed fair game that the order of the day for many writers was to turn nature "on its head." Some of these new works were based on new technologies recently founded, others were based on extrapolations of technologies whilst others tried to control nature by the power of man.

From the Earth to the Moon was a book written by Jules Verne in 1865. This was a book that showcased technology as a main aspect of its storyline. It is actually written about the Baltimore Gun Club and a group of gun enthusiasts. Interestingly, at the time the rise of gun weaponry was in full swing. From about 1855 until the end of the era in 1888, weapons were quickly being developed. In fact, throughout that time, eighteen different muskets or guns were created. It was a time when there was a huge focus on developing the best and most efficient arsenals. This focus on guns lays the backdrop of the novel.

> "I have now enumerated," said Barbicane, "the experiments which I call purely paper ones, and wholly insufficient to establish serious relations with the Queen of the Night. Nevertheless, I am bound to add that some practical geniuses have attempted to establish actual communication with her. Thus, a few days ago, a German geometrician proposed to send a scientific expedition to the steppes of Siberia. There, on those vast plains, they were to describe enormous

*geometric figures, drawn in characters of reflecting
luminosity, among which was the proposition regarding the
`square of the hypothe nuse,' commonly called the `Ass's
Bridge' by the French. `Every intelligent being,' said the
geometrician, `must understand the scientific meaning of that
figure. The Selenites, do they exist, will respond by a similar
figure; and, a communication being thus once established, it
will be easy to form an alphabet which shall enable us to
converse with the inhabitants of the moon."*

The gun club in the book attempts to make a sky-facing space gun
that can launch people into space. The goal is to land on the
moon. Although moon landings were a way away during the
Victorian era, people have dreamt about traveling into space since
the earliest civilizations. There are cave drawings dating back to
10,000 BC in Val Camonica, Italy that appear to have space
themes to them. It's a sign that people have always been
enthralled by what is beyond the Earth and how to reach it.
Because of the technological advancements of the nineteenth
century, it is likely that writers began to "dream bigger" than they
ever had. For the first time, discoveries were weighing in that
made things like "space guns to launch people to the moon" more
than just distant dreams.

In his book, the gun club also faces some obstacles: money,
excavation of a 900-foot deep hole that is 60-feet-wide, and
survival of the explosion needed to leave earth. The three main
obstacles are tackled with varying tools heavily based on real
technology. Though Verne wasn't completely accurate in his
speculated solutions, he was surprisingly close to what would
eventually materialize. His educated guesswork, though, bears
some congratulatory offerings. Due to the number of changes
happening in the real world, it was likely that Verne took his
scientific cues along with his imagination, to propose solutions. It
is because of the vast development of technology and new

discoveries that Verne was able to draw his own theories on how his obstacles could be overcome.

> "They began by investigating the state of their store of water and provisions, neither of which had suffered, thanks to the care taken to deaden the shock. Their provisions were abundant, and plentiful enough to last the three travelers for more than a year. Barbicane wished to be cautious, in case the projectile should land on a part of the moon which was utterly barren. As to water and the reserve of brandy, which consisted of fifty gallons, there was only enough for two months; but according to the last observations of astronomers, the moon had a low, dense, and thick atmosphere, at least in the deep valleys, and there springs and streams could not fail. Thus, during their passage, and for the first year of their settlement on the lunar continent, these adventurous explorers would suffer neither hunger nor thirst."

There are some signs though that Verne was using more imagination than fact. He describes the gravitational pull for space travel reaching a "neutral point." In reality, there is no such point; rather, gravity would not affect his travelers along any part of their trip. At the time "aether" was considered to be the way heat and light were both produced and it was included in Verne's writings. In reality, scientists Morley and Michelson dispelled the notion of aether in 1887 and rewrote the real creation of heat and light. Their theory eventually turned into the Theory of Relativity.

It is clear that technology, though not always accurate, played a big part in From the Earth to the Moon by Jules Verne. The time of the novel was 1865 when people were experiencing a boom in technological discoveries and were excited about new possibilities.

The book Twenty Thousand Leagues Under the Sea is a novel written by Jules Verne in 1870. It is filled with inventions that were created in the Victorian era. The focal point of the novel is the "sea monster," which turns out to be a submarine. The sub itself is powered through electricity, a technology that was discovered in 1819. It was Andre-Marie Ampere and Hans Christian Orsted who discovered electromagnetism and magnetic contact. In 1821, Michael Faraday invented a motor fueled by electric power. It is easy to see how prominent the discovery was by studying literature of the time.

"These reports arriving one after the other, with fresh observations made on board the transatlantic ship Pereira, a collision which occurred between the Etna of the Inman line and the monster, a proves verbal directed by the officers of the French frigate Normandie, a very accurate survey made by the staff of Commodore Fitz- James on board the Lord Clyde, greatly influenced public opinion. Light-thinking people jested upon the phenomenon, but grave practical countries, such as England, America, and Germany, treated the matter more seriously. In every place of great resort the monster was the fashion. They sang of it in the cafes, ridiculed it in the papers, and represented it on the stage. All kinds of stories were circulated regarding it. There appeared in the papers caricatures of every gigantic and imaginary creature, from the white whale, the terrible 'Moby Dick' of hyperborean regions, to the immense kraken whose tentacles could entangle a ship of five hundred tons, and hurry it into the abyss of the ocean. The legends of ancient times were even resuscitated, and the opinions of Aristotle and Pliny revived, who admitted the existence of these monsters, as well as the Norwegian tales of Bishop Pontoppidan, the accounts of Paul Heggede, and, last of all, the reports of Mr. Harrington (whose good faith no one could suspect), who

affirmed that, being on board the Castillan, in 1857, he had seen this enormous serpent, which had never until that time frequented any other seas but those of the ancient centuries."

In Twenty Thousand Leagues Under the Sea there is technology that was still not studied in depth by laymen. Yes, professionals were scrutinizing many new discoveries, but they had not yet reached the average middle-class in-home user level (unlike the novel, which had). This is part of the reason why literature focusing on aspects such as electricity was so welcomed by readers. Who wouldn't want to read about a technology that was "in the future"? Or, a technology that the wealthy or those in cities were privy to but the general middle and working classes were not.

In this novel, the submarine also carries out advanced research in the field of biology. Remember that when the novel was released, biology - as it is known today - was first being discovered. Marine biology was just beginning, too. It was Charles Darwin, from 1831 to 1836, who spent much of his time collecting marine specimens and organisms for study. It wasn't until later that century that a completely marine biology-centric study was done by Charles Wyville Thomson. The science itself was in its early stages so having it as a central theme in a common-to-the-day novel was a great attraction for avid readers. It only added to the mystery of science fiction within the book.

"From the 21st to the 23d of January, the Nautilus went at the rate of two hundred and fifty leagues in twenty-four hours, being five hundred and forty miles, or twenty-two miles an hour. If we recognized so many different varieties of fish, it was because, attracted by the electric light, they tried to follow us; the greater part, however, were soon distanced by

our speed, though some kept their place in the waters of the Nautilus for a time. The morning of the 24th, in 12° 5' south latitude, and 94° 33' longitude, we observed Keeling Island, a madrepore formation, planted with magnificent cocoas, and which had been visited by Mr. Darwin and Captain Fitzroy. The Nautilus skirted the shores of this desert island for a little distance. Its nets brought up numerous specimens of polypi, and curious shells of mollusca Some precious productions of the species of delphinulse enriched the treasures of Captain Nemo, to which I added an astraea punctifera, a kind of parasite polypus, often found fixed to a shell. Soon Keeling Island disappeared from the horizon and our course was directed to the north-west, in the direction of the Indian Peninsula."

Another feature of the book is the "transatlantic telegraph." The telegraph is another technology discovered in the Victorian era. It was 1837 when it was created by Samuel F. B. Morse. It is showcased in Twenty Thousand Leagues Under the Sea and the main characters Conseil, Ned Land and Aronnax get to see how it works firsthand as Captain Nemo uses it.

In the book, the visitors to the sub also use diving suits as they embark on shark hunts. Though the diving suit was actually created around 1710, the waterproof canvas needed to truly make the suit valuable wasn't developed until the 1830s by Charles Mackintosh. This is another technology that is used in the book and a sign of how Jules Verne was able to incorporate modern day advances into his works of fiction. It is another aspect of why his book was so popular. People liked reading about the new technology and what it could do. Most likely people reading were not in the position to even access a diving suit, so it created a deeper element of mystery and curiosity within readers.

"And Conscil, reassured, returned to the study of the bank, which the Nautilus was skirting at a moderate speed. There, beneath the rocky and volcanic bottom, lay out spread a living flora of sponges and reddish cydippes, which emitted a slight phosphorescent light, commonly known by the name of sea-cucumbers; and walking comatulse more than a yard long, the purple of which completely colored the water around. The Nautilus, having now passed the high bank in the Lybian Straits, returned to the deep waters and its accustomed speed."

Finally, Verne also mentions Matthew Fontaine Maury in his novel. Maury was well-known within the field of science as an oceanographer, among other professional pursuits. Born in 1806, he embarked on his career at 19 years old. His passion was studying the sea, and his system of chronicling oceanographic data was quickly adopted by both merchant marines and the navy. His findings were used to develop accurate charts and the means of navigating all major trade routes. The fact that he played a part in Twenty Thousand Leagues Under the Sea is a testament to how much technology was revered in the Victorian era. By making its way into novels of great importance and note, it is clear to see that the world was undergoing a huge developmental period in which changes for the better were many.

H. G. Wells penned The Time Machine in 1895, at the end of the Victorian era. He was able to gather a plethora of technological advancements and weave them into his writings. What is interesting is that he is intent on categorizing technology-versus-lack-of-technology in his novel. When using his time machine, the time traveler travels to a different era. He meets a people called Eloi. The Eloi have futuristic-looking buildings in which to function, but the buildings are falling apart. The Eloi see no need or want to repair them. Instead, they merely luxuriate while eating fruit. He takes one Eloi named Weena with him on his journey and she presents him with white flowers.

"The whole surface of the earth seemed changed— melting and flowing under my eyes. The little hands upon the dials that registered my speed raced round faster and faster. Presently 1 noted that the sun belt swayed up and down, from solstice to solstice, in a minute or less, and that consequently my pace was over a year a minute; and minute by minute the white snow flashed across the world, and vanished, and was followed by the bright, brief green of spring. The unpleasant sensations of the start were less poignant now. They merged at last into a kind of hysterical exhilaration. I remarked indeed a clumsy swaying of the machine, for which I was unable to account. But my mind was too confused to attend to it, so with a kind of madness growing upon me, I flung myself into futurity. At first I scarce thought of stopping, scarce thought of anything but these new sensations. But presently a fresh series of impressions grew up in my mind— a certain curiosity and therewith a certain dread— until at last they took complete possession of me. What strange developments of humanity, what wonderful advances upon our rudimentary civilization, I thought, might not appear when I came to look nearly into the dim elusive world that raced and fluctuated before my eyes! I saw great and splendid architecture rising about me, more massive than any buildings of our own time, and yet, as it seemed, built of glimmer and mist. I saw a richer green flow up the hill-side, and remain there, without any wintry intermission. Even through the veil of my confusion the earth seemed very fair. And so my mind came round to the business of stopping."

The protagonist also meets the Morlocks, who are ape-like creatures that live in underground darkness. Though they are in

that darkness, they have an industry and machinery knowledge
that lends itself to the betterment of the world above. The
Morlocks eventually steal the time machine that the main
character used to travel there and to return, he realizes that he has
to find it.

The time traveler decides that he needs to make a weapon to face
off against the Morlocks. He finds matches and creates a simple
weapon. The fact that he was able to create a weapon is proof that
at that time, many people were creating things. If there was some
purpose to fulfill and no tool was available, it was commonplace
to imagine, find raw materials and create something. Many
different guns were created throughout the Victorian era. Weapons
such as the Beaumont-Adams revolver of 1856, the Nordenfelt gun
of 1873 and the early machine-gun, the Garner gun of 1874, were
all new to the market. Out of necessity, the time traveler had to
create his own weapon that had a fire element to it. The fire he
creates allows him to get to the machine, but he ends up starting a
raging forest fire as he leaves.

*"At first, proceeding from the problems of our own age, it
seemed clear as daylight to me that the gradual widening of
the present merely temporary and social difference between
the Capitalist and the Labourer, was the key to the whole
position. No doubt it will seem grotesque enough to you—
and wildly incredible!— and yet even now there are existing
circumstances to point that way. There is a tendency to utilize
underground space for the less ornamental purposes of
civilization; there is the Metropolitan Railway in London, for
instance, there are new electric railways, there are subways,
there are underground workrooms and restaurants, and they
increase and multiply. Evidently, 1 thought, this tendency had
increased till Industry had gradually lost its birthright in the
sky. I mean that it had gone deeper and deeper into larger
and ever larger underground factories, spending a still-*

increasing amount of its time therein, till, in the end—! Even now, does not an East-end worker live in such artificial conditions as practically to be cut off from the natural surface of the earth? 'Again, the exclusive tendency of richer people— due, no doubt, to the increasing refinement of their education, and the widening gulf between them and the rude violence of the poor— is already leading to the closing, in their interest, of considerable portions of the surface of the land."

When the main character gets his time machine back, he travels 30 million years ahead of his time. When he arrives, he sees that life as it was known has died out. What life is left amounts to red crab-like animals and large butterflies. He starts moving through time incrementally, going farther and farther from his present day. As he moves, he sees the earth stop rotating and the sun dimming. He finally witnesses all life dying out.

Part of the interesting writing is the author's view of technology and its power. He obviously is conveying how exciting it is and how it gives humanity possibilities that it never had before. Wells considers technology to be a very powerful tool that can destroy humanity if not balanced. He presented the Eloi who had no ability to use technology; he presented the Morlocks who used technology but turned into monsters who couldn't face daylight. Another significant sign of Wells telling the reader how he felt were the white flowers Eloi Weena gave to the time traveler, with white symbolizing innocence. The Morlocks were in darkness, symbolizing death.

Another sign of how Wells felt about technology was his "fire" aspect. He created a fire-weapon that allowed him to leave. It was used for good so that he could return to his time machine and get out of that time. However, when he looked back he realized that his invention, or the technology he created, actually became a fierce weapon of mass destruction. This was a sign that he believed balance was a much-needed consideration for any technology entering the world.

It is evident that people of that time were seeing one new technological advancement after another. They were experiencing first-hand how powerful inventions were, and how they had the ability to change lives for the better. All three of these Victorian era novels are indicative of how quickly things were changing and how important the authors believed technology was to society. Whether it was heralding technology, as with Twenty Thousand Leagues Under the Sea, or cautioning people about technology as with The Time Traveler, writers had a lot to say about how advancements were affecting society as a whole.

The Invisible Man novella (1897)

Wells, who was hot on the success of The Time Machine and The Island of Doctor Moreau in this new era of technological thriller writing (something that would later morph into science-fiction as we know it today), produced The Invisible Man as a novella (short novel) in 1897. It would be serialized in Pearson's Weekly in the same year. The invisible man of the title is Griffin, a scientist who has devoted himself to research into optics and invents a way to change a body's refractive index to that of air so that it neither absorbs nor reflects light and thus makes the person invisible to the naked eye. He successfully carries out this procedure on himself, but later fails in his attempt to reverse it.

> *"The stranger came early in February, one wintry day, through a biting wind and driving snow, the last snowfall of the year, over the down, walking from Bramblehurst railway*

station, and carrying a little black portmanteau in his thickly gloved hand. He was wrapped up from head to foot, and the brim of his soft felt hat hid every inch of his face but the shiny tip of his nose; the snow had piled itself against his shoulders and chest, and added a white crest to the burden he carried. He staggered into the 'Coach and Horses' more dead than alive, and flung his portmanteau down. "A fire," he cried, "in the name of human charity! A room and a fire!" He stamped and shook the snow from off himself in the bar, and followed Mrs. Hall into her guest parlour to strike his bargain. And with that much introduction, that and a couple of sovereigns flung upon the table, he took up his quarters in the inn."

The story would be a cautionary tale of science experimentation going wrong and was set in the familiar backdrop of a quiet English village. Griffin (the protagonist), having rendered himself invisible with an earlier experiment, enters a village and sets up a lab in a room he rents in the village's only inn. He works night and day to come up with a formula that will reverse his invisibility. When he slips up and accidentally reveals himself, he engages in immature and violent actions until he is forced to run and find a new hiding place. As more people become aware of his existence, his situation becomes more perilous. Finally, he stumbles into the home of a former college professor whom he assumes will be interested in his experiments and willing to help him. His colleague, Mr. Kemp, however, reads newspaper accounts of Griffin's actions against people in the village and betrays his trust. Griffin is hunted down, caught and killed, whereupon he becomes visible again. The novella ends on a cliffhanger suggesting that Kemp might try his invisibility experiments now he is in possession of Griffin's work, though it is never answered as to whether this later happens.

Some believe that Arundel in Sussex, UK was the inspiration for the village that the Invisible Man runs amok in

"There wasn't anything there!" said Cuss, his voice running up into a shriek at the "there." "It's all very well for you to laugh, but I tell you I was so startled, I hit his cuff hard, and turned around, and cut out of the room - I left him -" Cuss stopped. There was no mistaking the sincerity of his panic. He turned round in a helpless way and took a second glass of the excellent vicar's very inferior sherry. "When I hit his cuff," said Cuss, "I tell you, it felt exactly like hitting an arm. And there wasn't an arm! There wasn't the ghost of an arm!" Mr. Bunting thought it over. He looked suspiciously at Cuss. "It's a most remarkable story," he said. He looked very wise and grave indeed. "It's really," said Mr. Bunting with judicial emphasis, "a most remarkable story."

Wells explored the extremes of human behavior within the book, not wanting to pigeonhole his work into any singular genre. He draws on the suspense of a thriller, the gothic of horror and the technology of what would later be known as science fiction; all of which are stuck into a melting pot of greatness that envelop the reader in a thrilling tale of the strange and wonderful, whilst setting the whole book in the familiar and vernacular English countryside. Wells himself was a well-read man and an amateur scientist, as so many of the gentry of Victorian society were. He knew what was fact and what was fiction, so much so that he could deploy the blur the line between the two in a far better manner than many of his peers; that way the works of Wells blend between these two to create a paradox that readers of the time simply would not have any experience in. This technique however did not isolate the reader, as the reader is drawn in with adventure, intrigue and mystery.

Wells actively acknowledged that the earlier works of Verne and Shelley (particularly Frankenstein) inspired many of his works, particularly The Invisible Man (which is a great literary connection to the roots of these two later Universal franchises). Wells likened Griffin to Frankenstein, aiming to play God in his pursuit of creating his own creature and to become God's superior by controlling nature. As with both tales, they have an important moral lesson as both do not go as the protagonist had hoped. Griffin's reckless actions of theft and deceit only make the reader less amenable to the lead character, and by the end of Well's tragic tale, we find that we have little sympathy for the character following his desperate and cruel actions. It all leaves the reader with one undeniable conclusion: the idea that scientific discovery must be controlled and not allowed to develop without adequate social or ethical control; an idea perhaps that is as crucial then as it is over 100 years later, today. The final chapter of the original book reads:

"And on Sunday mornings, every Sunday morning, all the

215

year round, while he is closed to the outer world, and every night after ten, he goes into his bar parlour, bearing a glass of gin faintly tinged with water, and having placed this down, he locks the door and examines the blinds, and even looks under the table. And then, being satisfied of his solitude, he unlocks the cupboard and a box in the cupboard and a drawer in that box, and produces three volumes bound in brown leather, and places them solemnly in the middle of the table. The covers are weather-worn and tinged with an algal green - for once they sojourned in a ditch and some of the pages have been washed blank by dirty water. The landlord sits down in an armchair, fills a long clay pipe slowly--gloating over the books the while. Then he pulls one towards him and opens it, and begins to study it--turning over the leaves backwards and forwards. His brows are knit and his lips move painfully. "Hex, little two up in the air, cross and a fiddle-de-dee. Lord! what a one he was for intellect!" Presently he relaxes and leans back, and blinks through his smoke across the room at things invisible to other eyes. "Full of secrets," he says. "Wonderful secrets "Once I get the haul of them—Lord! I wouldn't do what _he_ did; I'd just--well!" He pulls at his pipe. So he lapses into a dream, the undying wonderful dream of his life. And though Kemp has fished unceasingly, no human being save the landlord knows those books are there, with the subtle secret of invisibility and a dozen other strange secrets written therein. And none other will know of them until he dies."

The Invisible Man (1933)

"I'll show you who I am – and what I am!"

After the earlier successes of Dracula, Frankenstein, and The
Mummy, Universal and Carl Laemmle Jr. were keen to mine the
literary world for more gothic novels to add to their budding
monster franchise. James Whale, who was fresh from the success
of Universal's The Old Dark House with Boris Karloff based on the
novel Benighted, was swiftly appointed to work on the new
picture. Various ideas were thrown around until the production
settled on a work by the earlier writer H. G. Wells, called The
Invisible Man. This was however, not the first time that the
beloved book had been in production on Universal's lot. In fact,
Laemmle Senior had tried to make the picture many years earlier
but just could not get over the technology that would be required
to make an actor 'disappear' on screen. Nor could they find a
suitable story to make. Whale was unaware of the book's former
position at Universal, a position today that we might colloquially
term "development hell." Whale soon appointed R.C. Sherriff
who he brought specifically to Hollywood to pen the script of the
picture. Sherriff asked his staff to fetch a copy of the original book
so he could begin work right away. Instead of bringing him a
copy of the book they fetched a whole trunkload of unproduced
treatments and scripts to his office; it was then that he and Whale
discovered the true status of the movie at the studio. The
treatments varied from the sublime to the ridiculous and it was
quickly apparent to both men why the picture had never made it
into production. Scripts ranged from setting the action in Russia to
another set on a spacecraft on Mars. Instead, they handed back
the scripts to Universal's archives department, drove down to a
nearby second-hand bookstore, purchased a copy of the original
book and got to work. Unlike both Dracula and Frankenstein that

rely fully on the stage versions of the famous tales, the duo set out to create a script that did not divert too much from the original novel.

> "We'll begin with a reign of terror, a few murders here and there, murders of great men, murders of little men – well, just to show we make no distinction. I might even wreck a train or two... just these fingers around a signalman's throat, that's all."

While the script was finalized, Laemmle went ahead and offered the lead character's role to Karloff. Karloff by this time was a bankable star for the genre and Laemmle thought the movie needed a safe pair of hands at the helm. Karloff turned down the offer and worked on another project. He cited the fact that the actor playing the character is only seen at the very end of the film and thus it would be beneath him to enter into such a role. Laemmle reluctantly agreed and he with Whale started to look for another star to fill the invisible boots. Despite Whale and Karloff being friends and close work colleagues, Whale was not keen on having Karloff in the picture, so was glad Karloff had turned the role down; he said at the time he was looking for an actor who had more of a distinctive voice than he did in presence (in reference to Karloff's stature). Other sources stated that Whale wanted a more refined English actor to play the maniacal English scientist, one whose voice would be posher and would therefore suggest to the audience that he was more intellectual. Whale was walking the lot's soundstages one afternoon when he happened upon a screen test being undertaken for another picture. Walking past he heard an articulate and defined English accent echoing out of the stage. He turned in and watched the test of new-to-Hollywood actor Claude Rains. Rains, who had very little screen experience but bags of stage experience, had come to Hollywood to further his career. Whale immediately saw Laemmle, who pulled some strings and pulled Rains out of his commitments for this other picture and placed him straight into the lead role within Whale's Invisible Man.

"An invisible man can rule the world. Nobody will see him come, nobody will see him go. He can hear every secret. He can rob, and rape, and kill!"

To achieve the effect of the "unwrapping" scene and the invisibility scenes in general, Whale worked with John Fulton, John J. Mescall, and Frank D. Williams to create the special effects. They all considered an early attempt to undertake the process from a British Pathé production of The Shielding Window, in which they attempted to make items float in thin air to varying degrees of success. Whereas Werewolf of London had used editing to achieve the transformative scene, the filmmakers here decided to use optical tricks that could be used in any travelling magic show to achieve the scenes. Fulton deployed what was later called the "traveling matte" to achieve this: a moving mask that changes from frame to frame was used to cover part of an image in order to be replaced with another, a combination of a process camera and projectors. Rains would wear black velvet gloves, masks and tights, so as to not reflect light, he would then wear a secondary layer of clothes (that would remain visible), which would be far brighter in color. Rains would act to the camera in front of black velvet screen, and the scene would be recorded on a film negative in reverse making a matte. This would then be combined with other footage in a seamless way to give the impression of him disappearing. The process is actually not much different to this day where blue/green screens replace the black velvet and computers take over the rest of the process. The whole technique was quite ingenious for the time.

The makeup would also prove problematic for the production, not least for the leading actor. Pierce worked with Whale and the original source material of the novel to provide a look that is wholly described by one character from the original book. The heavy bandages that were applied to Rains' face ensured that he would have to act wholly blind in nearly all scenes and would have to breathe through a tube since no holes for eyes or air could be left, particularly for the close-up shots. A stunt double was used on particularly long days in order to give Rains some space to breathe and recover. Eagle-eyed viewers could spot that the double is noticeably shorter than Rains, so a lot of his scenes have been cut, though they are not altogether missing.

> "The drugs I took seemed to light up my brain. Suddenly I realized the power I held, the power to rule, to make the world grovel at my feet."

The movie would be produced in what is now called "pre-code Hollywood." This era of American film history is when sound first made its way into productions but before the rules of censorship came in around 1934. Although the initial code predated all movies as it was introduced in 1930, the code was not actively enforced until 1934; this afforded Whale greater opportunities to create a film that was not only more in keeping with the original but would also shock audiences in the scenes it needed to. That is why the movie pulls little punches and was surely a spectacular effect for 1930s audiences – to see a man disappear in front of their very eyes. H. G. Wells, the original writer of the novel, was wholly impressed when he first saw the picture in London. He praised the special effects and pacing, but was a little miffed at Whale's attempt to make Griffin into a heinous madman. He did not agree that the character should be turned into an untamed lunatic, though Whale pointed out that the character was not far from that point in the original text.

> *"Power, I said! Power to walk into the gold vaults of the nations, into the secrets of kings, into the Holy of Holies; power to make multitudes run squealing in terror at the touch of my little invisible finger. Even the moon's frightened of me, frightened to death! The whole world's frightened to death!"*

The movie was a great hit, exceeding the box-office expectations of Universal. Critics and audiences alike praised the movie's chill factor along with the amazing special effects. By the end of the year it was regarded as a "must see" and one of the top ten best films from that year (which is a high accolade considering how many pictures were released that year!). Whale was praised for the success of the picture by his peers. At the Venice Film Festival of the following year he would be honored with an award for the picture. Fulton would also be honored by an Academy Award nomination that year. Rains, who acted in his first ever Hollywood picture, would see his career take off and Universal would be quietly happy with the amassed box-office receipts that the picture brought them. The New York Times heaped particular praise on the movie:

> *"No actor has ever made his first appearance on the screen under quite as peculiar circumstance as Claude Rains does in the picturization of H. G. Wells's novel "The Invisible Man," which is the chief attraction at the Seventh Avenue Roxy. Other players have, it is true, been thoroughly disguised by weird makeup, but in this current offering Mr. Rains's countenance is beheld for a mere half minute at the close of the proceedings. The rest of the time his head is either*

completely covered with bandages or he is invisible, but his voice is heard. This eerie tale evidently afforded a Roman holiday for the camera aces. Photographic magic abounds in the production, the work being even more startling than was that of Douglas Fairbanks's old picture "The Thief of Bagdad." The story makes such superb cinematic material that one wonders that Hollywood did not film it sooner. Now that it has been done, it is a remarkable achievement. It was directed by James Whale, and R. C. Sherriff, author of "Journey's End," wrote the script. Although various incidents may be spine-chilling, it is a subject with a quota of well-turned comedy."

Rains' daughter many years later recalled that her father took her to see the picture in London one cold and dark wintery night at their local cinema. Wearing a long coat, thick scarf and fedora hat he approached the ticket window to buy two tickets, for the usher to reply that they could obviously enter for free being that he was in the picture and that he had come dressed in his costume. Her father laughed off the situation and would not enter until the usher had taken full payment for their two tickets.

The Invisible Man Returns (1940)

After the Laemmle's had left the company and the monster franchise had proved how profitable it still was, Universal looked again at the previous movies and decided that The Invisible Man was worthy of a sequel. What they would create would be regarded by many as on par with the original and a great addition to the Universal catalogue. Veteran film director Joe May was drafted in, and he set out to assemble a great team of cast and crew to do the picture justice.

"Willie Spears: Where are you? Where are you?

Geoffrey Radcliffe: Here beside you!

Willie Spears: But, but I can't see you!

Geoffrey Radcliffe: Of course you can't, I'm a ghost.

Willie Spears: [Gasps] Ghost!

Geoffrey Radcliffe: [Sneezes]

Willie Spears: What kinda ghosts sneeze?

Geoffrey Radcliffe: It's cold in the other world, so cold!"

The Curt Siodmak-penned script would be a straightforward escapist joy with some excellent twists. A wealthy coal mining executive (Geoffrey) would be accused of murder; a murder that he didn't do. He sends his fiancée to contact an old friend of his, Dr. Griffin (from the original) to help prove his innocence. Griffin agrees to help and travels to the prison to show them a formula he has created that makes a human invisible. But an unfortunate side effect of the drug is that is makes them mad. The convicted executive drinks the potion and soon escapes. As a wily inspector of Scotland Yard searches for the escaped convict, Griffin frantically searches for an antidote and Geoffrey frantically searches for the real killer. Time is short. Geoffrey is slowly but surely going insane and needs to prove his innocence before it is too late.

"There's a very small chance it will work and a far greater one that it will kill him. If I don't try it, he has no chance whatsoever."

The music of the picture was exceedingly high caliber for production. It was produced by Charles Previn and composers Hans Salter and Frank Skinner, who together produced an iconic score for this sequel. Special effects were achieved using the same team as last time, headed up by John Fulton. The film would also see Vincent Price take center stage in his first horror genre role, a role that he would not return to until the House of Wax in 1953, a role that would forever typecast him in the genre. A notable exception would be his voice-over cameo as the Invisible Man in Abbott and Costello Meet Frankenstein (1948), which technically made Price the only actor to play the cackling madman more than once. Jon Hall does play an invisible character in two different sequels, though they are two different characters, thus making either Price or Rains the true Invisible Man.

Sequels

The movie would again prove a popular hit for the studio making back almost three times what its original budget was. This would spawn a number of sequels, some comical and some serious. They include: The Invisible Woman (1940), Invisible Agent (1942), and The Invisible Man's Revenge (1944).

The Invisible Woman was a science fiction comedy addition to the series that was released near the end of 1940. It was more of a screwball comedy than other films in the series and was not popular with critics. The New York Times was pretty scathing in its review of the picture:

"Perhaps the maddest jape to have arrived hereabouts recently is "The Invisible Woman," currently causing eye strain at the Rialto. It is silly, banal and repetitious; it is essentially a two-reel comedy with elephantiasis and full of the trick disappearances and materializations that seemed new when "Topper" first came out. The script is as creaky as a two-wheeled cart and were it not for the fact that John Barrymore is taking a rid in it we hate to think what "The Invisible Woman" might have turned out to be."

The movie was in fact a big gamble at the time. Universal noted that comedy and horror pictures could be easily mashed together to produce a profitable picture, but they did however take a leap in the dark with this movie. They assigned a budget that was almost three times larger than any of their other B-movies and affixed a star of John Barrymore to the picture. Whether it was a combination of the need for some escapist joy or the curiosity of seeing a woman disappear we are unsure, though one thing is for certain; the public loved the film and made it highly profitable for the studio. The critics loathed the film but the public lapped it up, making it one of the top thirty highest-drawn box-office successes of 1940.

The success of The Invisible Woman led to Universal creating Invisible Agent in 1942, a movie that would be the summer hit of that year. The movie updated the franchise by bringing it into the modern day, a process that had been popular with some productions at the time (Basil Rathbone's Sherlock Holmes for example). This time the central character is the grandson of the original Invisible Man who is drafted in by the government to be deployed behind enemy lines to defeat the Nazis (just like Sherlock Holmes also was). Jon Hall started in the title role with Ilona Massey as his double-agent love interest, Maria Sorenson. Longtime Universal player Peter Lorre also completed the lineup as the piece's villain. Siodmak would again pen the script, often using his own experiences of being a refugee in Germany from years earlier. The movie was a morale booster for a country that had just joined the international struggle. It would motivate those serving abroad and at home, and would be more a heroic picture of courage than a typical monster flick.

> "Prof. Gibbs: If more women were invisible, life would be much less complicated.
>
> Richard Russell: And much less interesting."

Again, like the previous installments, the picture was a phenomenal success, proving once again Universal's shrewd moves to stay ahead of the times and give the people what they wanted. It was one of the first of the monster movies to claim a $1m turnover at the box-office; which Universal was incredibly proud of at the time. The movie again would be nominated for an Academy Award for its special effects. The critics once again despised the outing, however this did nothing to halt the rush of people to movie theaters across the country to see it.

The final true installment to the Invisible Man's franchise of movies would be The Invisible Man's Revenge (1944). Jon Hall provided the title character once more, but this time is cast as a different character (as previously mentioned). The story this time is one of revenge and theft; it contains suspense, murder and is altogether more dark in tone that the previous incarnations. A predictable plot is matched with lackluster performances that are overshadowed by camera trickery that had become more gimmicky than awe-inspiring. Initially, Universal approached Rains to come back for one final outing as his famous creation; he however politely declined, so Hall from the previous movie was cast instead.

"It must have been. Warped by imaginary wrongs. A man fighting shadows. He's to be pitied, really. He probed too deeply in forbidden places. What a man earns, he gets. Nature has a strange way of paying him back in his own coin."

The movie was a reasonable success but it was far less financially successful than the previous installments. The critics once again turned on the franchise and fewer members of the public saw the picture. Although this would be the final movie in the franchise, it would not be the final time that the character would be seen. Universal was in the throes of making both monster crossover movies and the "Abbott and Costello Meets" movies. The invisible joker would therefore turn up in Abbott and Costello Meet Frankenstein in 1948 and Abbott and Costello Meet the Invisible Man in 1951. Both of these were massively successful, particularly the former, which grossed well over $3m.

Abbott and Costello Meet the Invisible Man in 1951

"*Wilbur Grey: And another thing Mr. Chick Young! The next time I tell you that I saw something when I saw it, you believe me that I saw it!*

Chick Young: Oh relax. Now that we've seen the last of Dracula, the Wolf Man, and the Monster, there's nobody to frighten us anymore.

Invisible Man: Oh, that's too bad. I was hoping to get in on the excitement.

Chick Young: Who said that?

Invisible Man: Allow me to introduce myself. I'm the Invisible Man."

THE CREATURE FROM THE
BLACK LAGOON

Legends of the deep…

Tales of dark mysterious creatures lurking at the bottom of oceans and waterways have been with us for millennia. Originally told as verbal tales of forewarning, they would soon morph into fiction for entertainment purposes. Possibly it all started with Konrad Gesner. Gesner was a writer who was born in March of 1516. He was known as a physician and botanist. One of his contributions to the world of writing was his description of a sea monster called the "sea bishop." It was a curious creature he described, that had the body parts and characteristics of the Catholic clergymen called bishops. Whether or not the "sea bishop" was real, it gave way to more and more writings about creatures from deep in the waters - a place that was still unknown to the average reader.

There is a mystery about the water. Without intricate aids, humans can't stay underwater for extended periods of time. There is an entire world of creatures however, that can. They don't need any artificial assistance to make their homes in the deep. More and more writers began using the sea as the backdrop for their horror stories that included monsters living underwater. Here are some of the biggest names and titles that withstood the test of time to become highly respected novels of note.

Herman Melville's Moby Dick

Perhaps one of the best known books that features the sea monster is the epic novel Moby Dick by Herman Melville. The book was first published in 1851 and it recounts the fictional story of Ishmael as he travels with Captain Ahab. Ahab was on a previous voyage in which the white whale, named Moby Dick, caused him to lose a leg at the knee and to ruin his ship entirely. Upon first release and up until Melville's death in 1891, the book was largely thought to be a failure selling only 3,200 copies. It wasn't until the twentieth century that it found its place in American literature.

It took Melville a year and a half to pen the novel. He used such historical texts as the Bible and Shakespeare to shape his novel. What sets the novel apart from other stories is its amazingly realistic descriptions of events throughout the book. Whale hunting is not an easy task. Maneuvering on the sea isn't either. Melville manages to put into words the arduous struggles of the sea and the eventual face off with the giant sea monster. His desire for revenge carries him with a determination and laser-tight vision of what he will do when he and Moby Dick meet again.

The story begins simply with "Call me Ishmael." Those three words manage to perfectly introduce the stage upon which the story unfolds. The character decides to go on a voyage on the whaling ship the Pequod. Ship owners Peleg and Bildad tell Ishmael about Captain Ahab, describing him as a god-like character who commands the sea as if it serves him. An ode to the Bible comes when a character named Elijah prophesies Ishmael's fate if he joins the captain. Despite protestations, Ishmael departs on Christmas Day.

> *"And what thing soever besides cometh within the chaos of this monster's mouth, be it beast, boat, or stone, down it goes*
>
> *all incontinently that foul great swallow of his, and perisheth in the bottomless gulf of his paunch."*

Ishmael meets a range of characters who play their parts as crew members on the Pequod. Ahab finally makes his address to the crew, describing in no uncertain terms his quest: to gain revenge against the white whale. It is not with another man that he has his ill feelings; rather, it is against the whale Moby Dick. Throughout their adventure, they make contact with nine different ships. The crew members on each one are asked about the whale and potential sightings in an effort to continue tracking it through the sea.

What is key to Melville's tale is the central character—the whale. What other creature from the deep could elicit such intense and sustained feelings as those belonging to Captain Ahab? What creature of the sea could make a man focus his life's journey on its defeat? Likely no other sea beast than the famed Moby Dick. Throughout the story he consistently remains an elusive foe. Though Captain Ahab spots him more than a few times, it isn't until the end of the tale that he is able to engage in a true decision-making battle with the whale. As is appropriate to the formidable foe, however, Moby Dick ends up dragging Captain Ahab out of sight most likely to his timely end. The interesting thing about the novel is Captain Ahab's consistent goal of meeting with the whale and settling the score. In the end, he meets him but hardly to the end he had hoped.

Melville's Captain Ahab is faced with letting revenge motivate him and in the end, it kills him. Despite being an obvious expert at maneuvering a vessel and commanding a ship, that is never enough for him. He isn't willing to let the earlier encounter with the whale go. He sees the loss of his old boat and his leg as leaving a score to settle with a whale. Melville uses anthropomorphism to give the whale much more power than it should have. To fuel his story of revenge, the whale plays a knowing and intellectual part in the book. It's as if the whale knows what he did, what Ahab wants (to find him) and purposefully stays one step ahead of Ahab. He is able to taunt the captain with his quick movement and sly dexterity. Although this is not possible with an actual whale, to fuel the story's intent the whale takes on human characteristics.

> "Mad with the agonies he endures from these fresh attacks,
> the infuriated Sperm Whale rolls over and over; he rears his
>
> enormous head, and with wide expanded jaws snaps at
> everything around him; he rushes at the boats with his head;
> they are propelled before him with vast swiftness, and
> sometimes utterly destroyed."

Melville wrote this story in 1851 when marine life was still being studied. Like the other two writers featured, Hugo and Verne, Melville uses the unknown and mysterious characteristics of sea creatures to captivate the audience. Of course he takes his writing a step farther and anthropomorphizes his whale, but he still played upon people's general lack of knowledge of what whales truly are capable of. Although whales in the ocean cannot plan and plot, or make decisions to taunt, it made fantastic content for one of the greatest sea monster novels of all time. Moby Dick is included in the best novels ever created due to its themes, its writing style and its powerful characters, a main one of which is the white whale. He is the center of most of the conflict within the story.
Throughout the entire story Captain Ahab is seeking him. In fact, that is the reason why he embarks on his journey. He follows him relentlessly to settle some score that the whale represents. By using the whale as the enemy, Melville is able to convey the longstanding reputation of a sea creature as dangerous, mysterious and powerfully destructive.

Victor Hugo's Toilers of the Sea

Another novel that featured creatures from the deep was Victor

Hugo's Toilers of the Sea. The book was published in 1866 and is set on an island village. Like Moby Dick, the story tells the tale of an ominous sea creature that tests the people sailing. What is notable about this creature is that he is very much true to the actual animal. In Melville's Moby Dick, the whale seems to stay one-step ahead of Ahab, almost with a mindful intent of keeping Ahab following him without respite. The octopus of Toilers of the Sea is much more wild and without forethought. He is merely a giant octopus, scary and strong, but hardly of the reasoning capabilities that Moby Dick seemed to possess.

The story of Toilers of the Sea follows Gilliat, a boy who becomes a fisherman and avid sailor. It all starts innocently enough when a girl named Deruchette writes Gilliat's name in the snow. He sees it and becomes enamored with the girl. He eventually falls in love with her. She is the niece of steamship owner Mess Lethierry whose boat is named Durande. The captain of the ship, Sieur Clubin, sets in motion a plan to cause the ship to sink when on the Hanois reef. His plan is to find safety with a band of Spanish smugglers called the Tamaulipas. He meets with a swindler named Rantaine; Rantaine had earlier stolen money from Mess Lethierry. Clubin robs Rantaine of money at gunpoint.

Clubin then directs the boat towards the Hanois Reef as planned. His goal is to reach it, swim out to shore, team up with the smugglers and then appear as if he drowned. He will have the money and freedom to live his life anywhere he pleases. Unfortunately, his plan doesn't work as he hoped. Due to intense fog, he mistakes Hanoi reef for Douvres reef, which leaves him still halfway between France and the city in which he started out, Guernsey. He spies a cutter and jumps into the water to try to catch it. It is here that something grabs his leg and pulls him down to his death.

When the town hears about the wreck, ship owner Mess Lethierry wants to get the Durande's engine returned. Deruchette commits to marrying whichever sailor is able to successfully bring back the engine to her uncle. Mess Lethierry confirms the matching and says that whoever brings it back will surely have her hand in marriage. Gilliat decides this is his mission. He fearlessly embarks on his journey to find the engine and gain Deruchette as his wife.

"No wild beast can compare with the sea for mangling its prey. The waves are full of talons. The north wind bites, the billows devour, the waves are like hungry jaws. The ocean strikes like a lion with its heavy paw, seizing and dismembering at the same moment."

Throughout his journey, Gilliat endures many struggles. He fights the frigid sea temperatures. He fends off hunger and thirst. One of his biggest battles however is his struggle against a large octopus that nearly causes his end. The octopus is described as a large creature with great tentacles that pull him down powerfully. Author Victor Hugo created ink wash paintings of the creature to illustrate its formidable power. In his artwork, Hugo showcases a deep black octopus with tentacles straining wildly in its underwater habitat. Its head is large and bulbous but the way he depicts the eight long arms is what creates the scary form of the sea creature.

In the end Gilliat is able to just barely fend off the octopus. He manages to also return the engine to the owner. Although Lethierry wishes to honor his promise of Deruchette's hand in marriage, she accepts a marriage proposal from a priest, Ebenezer Caudry, who recently came to their town. The wedding is held quickly and they leave town on a ship called the Cashmere. Gilliat ends up waiting for the tide on a rock. As he watches the Cashmere sail out to sea, he eventually allows the tide to wash him away and engulf him. He drowns.

The same theme of dangerous and mysteriously dark sea creatures is alive in this story as in Moby Dick. At the time, marine life was just starting to be studied and people still understood animals in the sea to be a secret—at times dangerous secrets. Hugo's tale is not a hopeful one and the underwater sea creature symbolizes another struggle that the protagonist of the story has to face. Everything for Gilliat is filled with suffering and woe. Though he is hopeful at the beginning, after his encounter with the sea, he is left without that hope. He is ready to allow the sea to overcome him and take him away. Much like Captain Ahab of Moby Dick, he is carried away into the unknown and engulfed by the waters.

Creature From The Black Lagoon (1954)

The legend...

> "I can tell you something about this place. The boys around here call it 'The Black Lagoon'; a paradise. Only they say nobody has ever come back to prove it..."

The Amazon River in South America is the largest river (by volume of water) in the world, and according to many it is also the longest river in existence. Spanning almost entirely across the whole continental width of South America, the river is vast and its depths are huge. There are areas and territories to this day that are still being explored and new species of animals being discovered. Rooted in the history of the countries it passes through, it has an ancient tale to tell that by all accounts is still being told to us today. It was the year 1500 when Spanish conquistador Vicente Yáñez Pinzón became the first documented European to sail into the river. Another Spanish explorer, Francisco de Orellana, was the first European man to travel from the sources situated in the Andes down to the mouth of the river. During his journey, Orellana named some of the affluents of the Amazonas, such as the Rio Negro, the Rio Napo and the Rio Jurua. The name "Amazonas" came from the native warriors that attacked this expedition. They were mostly women, and reminded Orellana of the woman warriors called the Amazons from the Hellenic culture. It would these events that would spark countless legends and tales for many years to come.

Explorers and sailors alike would bring back tales of dread and foe surrounding the vast and mysterious Amazon River. "El Tunchi" is an evil spirit that haunts the jungle and terrorizes people with a shrieking sound. Explorers who had witnessed the creature say he's a composite of all the dead found in the surrounding rainforest, while other legends describe him as the ghost of a man who became lost and died in the jungle. "El Lobizon" is a werewolf that supposedly stalks the shores of the river near the main rainforests. Stories of this creature abound throughout all of Central and South America. It is described as half-man and half-wolf, with red eyes and razor-sharp teeth. Unlike the more European legends of the werewolf, you cannot transform into said beast when bitten. Instead, the seventh son of any family has the power within his genes to turn into the beast at will. The beasts that were spotted with their glowing red eyes could easily have been local wolves, or so they say…

The mighty Amazon River

As with El Lobizon, the next myth evolved from true accounts. "Bufeo Colorado," or pink river dolphins, are found only in the Amazon, and considering their unusual appearance and intelligence it's no wonder there's a whole raft of tales associated with this peculiar creature. One such legend tells of a dolphin who shape-shifts into an attractive fisherman. He uses his charm to lure girls away and convince them to have sex with him. If he succeeds, the girl becomes pregnant and gives birth to a pink dolphin. The legend is that the only way to make the man-dolphin return to being his watery mammal self is to make him fall from a great height.

A more natural legend but just as terrifying is that of the pirarucu, which is a real fish that grows to humongous proportions. Some specimens have been found to be over 10ft in length and weigh close to 500 pounds. The fish are covered in thousands of metallic-like scales that are so tough that the forest tribes kill the fish to make arrowheads out of their sharp scales. The same natives tell tales of how the fish was once a human warrior from a

southwestern tribe who was brave but heartless. The story goes
that he angered the gods and they transformed him into an
immortal fish that swims the length and breadth of the river as an
eternal punishment. The fish supposedly exacts his revenge on the
locals by attacking and killing anyone who swims in his way.

Perhaps one of the most interesting additions to the myths from
this area is the "Mapinguari," the Amazonian version of Big Foot
or the Sasquatch. It aggressively pursues all human hunters who
venture into the deep rainforests of the central basin. It is said to
have large armadillo feet, a single large red eye, and a huge
gaping mouth in its stomach. It is covered in thick fur and makes
howling shrieks that can be heard for miles around.

The movie

The interest of producer William Alland was further piqued when
at a dinner party in 1941 he was told a mysterious tale about
creatures from the Amazon River. Sitting next to famed Mexican
cinematographer Gabriel Figueroa at a gala dinner heralding the
new movie Citizen Kane, Figueroa spoke of a colleague of his that
had recently gone missing. He explained that a documentary
maker he knew back in Mexico City had been told a tale of half-
men-half-fish living in a small and remote section of the Amazon
River. He had researched his trip and won backers for an
expedition/documentary. After several weeks, no contact had
been made with the team of filmmakers. Some time passed after
they were due to return and a search team was sent out, but they
never found them. Figueroa recounted this information to Alland
who was enthralled by the tale. After the gala he researched the
story but found very few facts to back it up, and instead he wrote a
small treatment some years later entitled "The Sea Monster."

A decade later, Alland was working at Universal Studios as a producer. He had been brought in and had assembled a team of professionals to turn out flicks geared particularly towards the emerging market of baby boomer teenagers. He had mixed success but it was the more thrill-and-chill lead movies that seemed to chime at the box-office. The Black Castle (1952) and It Came From Outer Space (1953) were very successful, and Universal asked Alland to center his next picture around one of their classic monsters. Alland declined, stating that although he adored the classic monsters, he felt that their stories had been played out numerous times and that a new monster for a new atomic age should be brought into the stable. It was at this moment that he recalled the treatment he had written years earlier. Set in a romantic, tropical environment that had the dynamics of water and steam-powered boats and a murderous monster background, he realized he might have found a winning formula.

"There are many strange legends in the Amazon. Even I, Lucas, have heard the legend of a man-fish."

He worked further on his old treatment, making the story more akin to Beauty and the Beast or King Kong, whilst adding various new elements that he had dreamt up. He gathered help in 1952 in the form of Maurice Zimm who expanded the story with the aid of Harry Essex and Arthur Ross. The treatment grew from The Sea Monster to The River Dweller to, finally, The Creature from the Black Lagoon. Universal loved the new script and immediately asked Alland to get the picture into production. It was at this point, following the success of the 3D film House of Wax in 1953, that Jack Arnold was hired to direct the film in the same format. 3D had been increasingly experimental and popular throughout the early 1950s with Alfred Hitchcock using the process for his movie Dial M for Murder in 1954. However, it would be Vincent

Price's House of Wax that would shock audiences around the world and set the new method of movie presentation off on its first (and not last!) phase of fad-like use.

Director Jack Arnold claimed that his main goal in the making of the picture was to create a sense of dread. He said at the time:

"It plays upon a basic fear that people have about what might be lurking below the surface of any body of water. You know the feeling when you are swimming and something brushes your legs down there - it scares the hell out of you if you don't know what it is. It's the fear of the unknown. I decided to exploit this fear as much as possible."

Designing the Creature for its thrill factor, and the practicality factor of actually swimming under water would prove the two biggest challenges of the picture. The Creature would go through various designs to get the right one to use on the big screen. Initially Alland wanted a melancholic looking beast that was a kind of mutated human where the face and features would be human but fish-like. He wanted audiences to be frightened by the fact that the monster could be human at first glance but actually fish-like in appearance. This design was changed to a more eel-like character that was sleek and slithery, something that could play well to the use of the new 3D technology. However, this was later changed due to the practicalities of making it swim. It would fall to former Disney Studios illustrator Millicent Patrick to create the now-iconic design of the Creature. Unfortunately, her role in the creation of the Creature would be deliberately downplayed by makeup artist Bud Westmore, who for over fifty years would receive sole credit for the Creature's conception.

Constructing the makeup and costume would be problematic. It would be fabricated from an airtight, molded sponge and rubber covering, which at the time cost slightly shy of $15,000. The head would be removable in emergencies and the suit would be fitted with air hosing that allowed the actor to breathe when filming underwater sequences. The suit would also be painted bright yellow to film some sequences filmed underwater as the black and white film would struggle to clearly define the figure as he swam to his next victim. Jack Kevan who had designed the costumes for The Wizard of Oz (1939) was brought in to make the final design, with Universal's Chris Mueller, Jr. sculpting the final headpiece.

Ben Chapman played the part of the Creature for the majority of the movie, with filming taking place at Universal's expansive backlot. Florida would be home to a number of other watery sequences, in particular Rice Creek near Palatka, which is now a state park. His costume was constructed in such a way that made it impossible for him to sit at any time, as he would be in it for more than 14 hours every day. It would often overheat, and he would spend most of time between takes bobbing around in the backlot's Fall's Lake. Shouts would often be heard from him, with him asking to be helped out or to be hosed down due to overheating. The vision through the mask was also poor and he scraped his co-star Julie Adam's face twice during production when carrying her.

Further filming also took place in nearby Jacksonville on the south side of the river near the old Acosta Bridge. It was here that the suit was worn by Ricou Browning (who was an accomplished swimmer) and painted yellow as the brackish waters were very dark in coloration. Ricou Browning, a professional diver and swimmer, was required to hold his breath for up to four minutes at a time for his underwater scenes as the Creature. The director's logic was that the air should travel through the monster's gills and he didn't want air bubbles to be shown emanating from Browning's mouth or nose. The costume was designed without an air tank initially, to add to the realism of the character. In subsequent films, this detail was ignored and air can be seen escaping from the top of the Creature's head. Browning recounts a fun encounter he had during production where he startled two passers-by. Desperate for the toilet following a scene wrapping, he swam to a nearby shore where he knew a temporary bathroom had been located. He came ashore (in full makeup) to where a passing mother and daughter happened to be walking. They saw him and they ran one way, he saw them and ran to the bathroom – just in time. The production crew never did find the couple to explain the sighting.

Falls Lake at Universal's backlot now complete with blue screen to the rear

Other notable stars attached to the project would be Richard Carlson and Julia Adams in the lead roles. It would be Adam who recounted later that no matter what movies she made later or how great her acting was, she felt she was always labeled "The actress from the Creature movie."

The reviews of the movie upon release were all positive and audiences flocked to the cinemas to see "the creature feature" on March 5, 1954. Variety said:

"The 3-D lensing adds to the eerie effects of the underwater footage, as well as to the monster's several appearances on land. The below-water scraps between skin divers and the prehistoric thing are thrilling and will pop goose pimples on the susceptible fan, as will the closeup scenes of the scaly, gilled creature. Jack Arnold's direction does a firstrate job of developing chills and suspense, and James C. Havens rates a good credit for his direction of the underwater sequences. Richard Carlson and Julie Adams co-star in the William Alland production and carry off the thriller very well. As befitting the Amazonian setting, Adams appears mostly in brief shorts or swim suits."

The movie was a massive hit, raking in over $1.3million on a very modest B-movie budget. This was fortunate, as while the original script was being worked on, it would be agreed that a sequel would be needed. To this end, the condition of the Creature at the end of the movie was unknown.

Revenge of the Creature (1955)

Using the working titles of Return of the Creature and Return of the Creature from the Black Lagoon, Universal was keen to get the gilled maniac back onto the big screens. Alland was back, along with the head of the production, John Arnold, to tell the follow-up tale to the monster hit. Principal photography took place at Marineland, Florida, which played the part of the film's Ocean Harbor Oceanarium. The St. Johns River that flows through this part of Florida would stand in for the Amazon River of this picture.

Various sets and disused restaurants were used to film the

production in Jacksonville (most of which were destroyed in a fire in 1962). One of the former restaurants would prove problematic for the production as the heat from the lighting rigs caused the set's temperature to overheat, which caused the sprinklers to start. The rush of sprinkled water ruined the equipment and drenched a number of extras, resulting in a few days being lost to the tight production program. The movie would also be the very first screen appearance of a very young, fresh-faced Clint Eastwood.

The tanks at Marineland, Florida now house performing dolphins

There were other setbacks to the production too. Actor/stuntman Tom Hennesy almost drowned during production. Playing the Creature in full makeup, he grabbed Helen Dobson (actually stuntwoman Ginger Stanley) on a pier and jumped with her into the river. The scene was shot at night, and when Hennesy and Stanley hit the water, they discovered it was full of jellyfish that had washed in with the nearby current - a current that was very strong. Hennesy let go of Stanley, who swam to the surface, but Hennesy's inflexible Gill-Man costume had become waterlogged and too heavy to fight the strong current. He was rescued by two local boys who happened to be watching the filming from a nearby boat, who quickly raced over and pulled him in. Hennesy, years later, recounted that if it weren't for the two boys being situated near to the set, he probably would have died that night.

The movie was again a huge hit with the public when it was released in 1955, grossing over $1m. The budget had been smaller, and lessons learnt from the previous film resulted in a more streamlined process. Critics were less than impressed with the sequel but praised its use of 3D, which had audiences rushing to the local theaters.

The Creature Walks Among Us (1956)

Alland would produce one final movie in this trilogy with a largely new crew. It would be entitled The Creature Walks Among Us and would be based around the premise of a scientist capturing the Creature and turning him into an air-breather, only for him to escape and start a killing rampage. The Creature, who had survived the first two movies, would be back for this final outing, though not in 3D. The underwater scenes were filmed at Wakulla Springs in North Florida, today a state park. Other locations in Florida were also utilized for location shooting. The movie was released in 1956 to mixed reviews but it made reasonable gains on its modest budget.

> "...because we all stand between the jungle and the stars, at a crossroads. I think we better decide what brings out the best in humankind, and what brings out the worst, because it's the stars or the jungle."

The St. Johns River in Florida where a number of scenes were shot

Legacy

The Creature was a hugely popular character of the Universal Monster lineup and although he came much later into the fray, he would become as popular as the other blockbuster monsters from the earlier decades.

The Creature was the star of Creature from the Black Lagoon: The Musical, a live performance show that was added to the Universal Studios Hollywood theme park in Los Angeles, California. It debuted on July 1, 2009 and closed down on March 9, 2010 being replaced by the Special Effects Stage, which opened three months later on June 26, 2010.

The Creature could also hold the accolade of being the most times a franchise has attempted to be remade by Universal. In 1982 John Landis would try to persuade executives and the former director of the original, Jack Arnold, to reboot the series. A script was completed that contained two Creatures. The proposed return of the Creature would also tie-in to the late 70s/early 80s return of 3D movies in theaters. Universal would ultimately decline and instead put their efforts into a third installment in the popular Jaws franchise (which was also presented in 3D). In 1992 John Carpenter toyed with the idea of remaking the original with Universal, as he had offices located on the backlot. A new script was commissioned and Peter Jackson was offered the director's chair. The project would again fall through.

Later in 1996 Ivan Reitman was planning a remake of his own, but the project would never come to fruition. Then in 1999 the remake came very close to happening following the success of The Mummy. Universal liked the idea but decided to plough ahead with a sequel to the summer blockbuster instead. In 2001 a story emerged in the local Hollywood presses that Arthur A. Ross, the original writer of the first movie, had written his own remake and was trying to get backing for the project. In 2002 Guillermo del Toro was attached to direct a new version, then he was replaced in October 2005 by Breck Eisner. This version would ultimately be canceled, though it had some great plot points of making the movie more akin to a modern day horror movie and reinventing the Creature's back story. Instead of being an ancient evolutionary quirk, he would instead be an industrial accident gone wrong with big corporations trying to cover-up his murderous escapades. The project was perhaps the closest to being brought to the big screen as it had a full working script, costume design and all the locations had been fully scouted. Four more attempts were made between 2007 and 2014 to bring the Creature to a cinema near you, all of which were ultimately shelved, even the one that had Scarlett Johansson tied to the lead role.

A production still from the original Creature From the Black Lagoon

ABOUT THE AUTHOR

Christopher Ripley was born in the UK but has been traveling to and living in the US for many years. He has been attending both Universal Studios Florida and Hollywood for over 20 years. He authored his first book in 2015, Halloween Horror Nights: The Unofficial Story & Guide, which went on to become a bestseller.

Since then he has setup the popular HHN blog hhnunofficial.com, become a co-presenter of the Scarezone podcast (a dedicated HHN pod- cast) and Dis After Dark (Europe's most downloaded Florida theme parks podcast), has ghostwritten a number of books and articles, and has other books in the pipeline, all related to Universal Studios.

His 2016 edition of the Survivor's Guide to Universal Studios' Halloween Horror Nights is currently available from Amazon and all other retailers.

You may also like...

Made in the USA
Middletown, DE
07 September 2020